The Long-Awaited One

A 30-Day Journey Through the Prophecies of the Coming Messiah

By Pauline Williams

ISBN 978-1-7028-1431-7

Table of Contents

Introduction

I love Christmas! I love Christmas trees and Christmas cards. I love Christmas cookies and candies (even if my hips don't!) From the music to the lights to the decorations to the celebrations with family and friends, it truly is my favorite time of the year. Most of all, I love the reason for the season, my Savior.

Over the years, our family has developed lots of fun traditions to make sure we never forget the true reason we celebrate Christmas. From the very beginning with our children, we have read the Christmas story before opening presents. It became an important right-of-passage for them to do the reading when they were old enough. We've always placed numerous nativity scenes around the house. We decorate the Christmas tree as a family, positioning the angels at the top and nativity ornaments in prominent places. We even gave the children miniature Christmas trees to put in their rooms. From participating in Operation Christmas Child to giving gifts through Angel Tree, we especially emphasized giving throughout the season as well. We worked diligently to ensure that our children grasped that Christmas is about more than gifts and decorations. It's about Jesus.

One of our favorite traditions was using an Advent calendar each year to count down the days to Christmas. When our children were little, we would buy the calendars with chocolates behind the doors, always a favorite. Later, we learned to make our own chocolates, and we would wrap them and place them in a wooden Advent calendar we had received as a gift. It was a beautiful Christmas tree-shaped wall hanging with small doors that we would open each of the 25 days of December. Inside each door was a small wooden ornament that hung on the knob of each door. It was a great way to build the anticipation and excitement.

One year, I decided it was time to add another element to the Advent calendar tradition. I wanted to bring attention to the prophecies throughout the Bible that pointed toward the coming of the Messiah and how Jesus fulfilled those promises. So, I scoured my Bible for the passages I had marked where the Messiah was prophesied. I took the list, put them in order, and placed them on strips of paper inside the doors of our Advent calendar. It was a great devotional reading plan leading up to Christmas. When my children were teenagers, I also had them read from Josh McDowell's book, *A Ready Defense*. There is a wonderful chapter in the book called, "Messianic Prophecies Fulfilled in Jesus," that details God's plan to send the Messiah. It truly set up the reading plan in a powerful way.

The whole reading plan provided such a great devotional time for us that I have taken the last year to organize the plan and add some resources for all of you. So, here it is - the Bible reading plan including devotional readings, discussion questions, and family activities. On the next page, I've described how to use each part of these resources. I pray that as you implement the reading plan each day, your heart will be filled with joy and wonder at how amazing God's plan for our redemption truly is. How incredible it is that God would send His one and only Son for us. So, celebrate this Christmas! Hang those lights, decorate that tree, and give those gifts. All the while, focus on the One who sacrificed heaven's glory to be Emmanuel, "God with us." The One who came to die for our sins and rise again to give us hope and a future.

How to use this book

#1 - For Everyone - Use the Bible Reading Plan.

- Read the passages individually or as a family read-aloud. The passages can be read from your favorite Bible translation, or you can use the verses as they are printed in the devotionals and activity sections. All of the verses in the devotional section are printed from the New International Version. All verses in the activity section are printed in the New International Reader's Version.

- We would encourage using the verses in conjunction with an Advent calendar or candle. Our family placed the Bible references behind the door of our Advent calendar which I described in the introduction. The kids would pull out the ornament, the scripture reference, and a piece of chocolate. Then they would look up the verses for the day. It became a favorite tradition in December.

- If you only have time for the daily Bible readings, that's fine. When I developed the plan, that was all we did. The cumulative effect of seeing the prophecies over the time leading up to Christmas was very powerful. God's Word promises that it will speak for itself:

Isaiah 55:10-11

As the rain and the snow
come down from heaven,
and do not return to it
without watering the earth
and making it bud and flourish,
so that it yields seed for the
sower and bread for the eater,
so is my word that goes out
from my mouth:
It will not return to me empty,
but will accomplish what I desire
and achieve the purpose for
which I sent it.

- There are 30 days of Bible readings. The first 25 lead up to the celebration of Christmas Day. The others are follow-up readings and can be used right after Christmas or saved to kick-off the new year.

#2 - For Adults and Teens - Use the devotional readings with the Bible readings.

- The devotionals are written to compliment the Bible readings which are included on the page or can be read from your favorite Bible.

- The Bible readings are broken-down into topics. At the beginning of each topic, there is a page dedicated to taking notes on the key words, character qualities, and events that are revealed in each passage. Then, as you complete each section, you can look back at all that you have learned.

#3 - For Adults, Teens, and Small Groups - Use the discussion questions to go deeper into the readings and devotionals.

- The questions are included to foster family or small group discussions about the readings.

#4 - For Parents and Children - Use the Activity section to bring the readings to life.

- The activity ideas and discussion questions are designed to be very flexible and can be done daily, weekly, or randomly as you choose one or two per topical section. Most of all, do not let them add stress to your Christmas! Only use the activities that fit your family's schedule.

- The discussion questions can be done formally or on the go. God tells us in Deuteronomy 6:7 that as parents we can "talk about them when you sit at home and when you walk along the road, when you lie down and when you get up."

- We plan to develop social media sharing pages to allow families to share the activities they develop to enhance the study. That way we can all encourage one another! Check for the links at paulinesmusic.com

#5 - For Everyone - Enjoy the Christmas music as a part of your celebration

- The music has been written to highlight the themes of the prophecies while celebrating the event of Jesus' birth. Some standard Christmas carols have been included as well. So, enjoy the music as a unit or mix it into your favorite Christmas playlist.

- To get your free download of the Christmas music go to *The Long-Awaited One* page at paulinesmusic.com.

The Long-Awaited One
Bible Reading Plan

The Prophecies

Day 1 (Messiah) – Genesis 3:15; 12:1-3
Day 2 (Messiah) – Psalm 118:21-23; Isaiah 28:16
Day 3 (Messiah) – Isaiah 11:1-5,10; Isaiah 16:5
Day 4 (Messiah) – Psalm 110:1-4
Day 5 (Messiah) – Isaiah 9:2,6-7
Day 6 (Birth) – Isaiah 7:14
Day 7 (Birth) – Micah 5:2-5a
Day 8 (Life) – Isaiah 61:1-3
Day 9 (Life) – Psalm 118:26-28; Zechariah 9:9
Day 10 (Death) – Zechariah 11:12-13;13:7; Psalm 41:9
Day 11 (Death) – Psalm 22:1,7-8,16-18
Day 12 (Death) – Exodus 12:3,5-7,12-14,46
Day 13 (Death) – Isaiah 52:13-15
Day 14 (Death) – Zechariah 12:10-13:1
Day 15 (Death & Resurrection) – Matthew 12:38-40

Day 16 (Resurrection) – Psalm 16:8-11
Day 17 (Resurrection) – Isaiah 60:1-3; Malachi 4:2
Day 18 (Resurrection) – Hosea 13:14
Day 19 (Salvation) – Isaiah 53
Day 20 (Messenger) – Malachi 3:1; Isaiah 40:3-5;
Day 21 (Messenger) - Luke 1:5-25

The Events

Day 22 (Angel to Mary) – Luke 1:26-56
Day 23 (John the Baptist) – Luke 1:57-80
Day 24 (Angel to Joseph) – Matthew 1:18-25
Day 25 (Jesus is born!) – Luke 2:1-20

The Follow-up

Day 26 (Messiah) – Luke 2:21-39
Day 27 (Wise Men) – Psalm 72:10-11; Matthew 2:1-12
Day 28 (Egypt) – Hosea 11:1; Matthew 2:13-15
Day 29 (Salvation) – Ezekiel 36:24-29a
Day 30 (Coming Again!) – Daniel 7:13-14

Long-Awaited One Reproducible Reading Plan

Day 1	Genesis 3:15; 12:1-3	**Day 16**	Psalm 16:8-11
Day 2	Psalm 118:21-23; Isaiah 28:16	**Day 17**	Isaiah 60:1-3; Malachi 4:2
Day 3	Isaiah 11:1-5,10-12; Isaiah 16:5	**Day 18**	Hosea 13:14
Day 4	Psalm 110:1-4	**Day 19**	Isaiah 53
Day 5	Isaiah 9:2,6-7	**Day 20**	Malachi 3:1; Isaiah 40:3-5
Day 6	Isaiah 7:14	**Day 21**	Luke 1:5-25
Day 7	Micah 5:2-5a	**Day 22**	Luke 1:26-56
Day 8	Isaiah 61:1-3	**Day 23**	Luke 1:57-80
Day 9	Psalm 118:26-28; Zechariah 9:9	**Day 24**	Matthew 1:18-25
Day 10	Psalm 41:9; Zechariah 11:12-13; 13:7	**Day 25**	Luke 2:1-20
Day 11	Exodus 12:3,5,7,12-13,46	**Day 26**	Luke 2:21-39
Day 12	Psalm 22:1,7-8,16-18	**Day 27**	Psalm 72:10-11; Matthew 2:1-12
Day 13	Isaiah 52:13-15	**Day 28**	Hosea 11:1; Matthew 2:13-15
Day 14	Zechariah 12:10-13:1	**Day 29**	Ezekiel 36:24-29a
Day 15	Matthew 12:39-40	**Day 30**	Daniel 7:13-14

Bible Reading Notes Days 1 - 5

The Promised Messiah...

<u>Genesis 3:15</u>

- Satan will be permitted to hurt the promised Messiah
- The Messiah will win in the end

<u>Genesis 12:1-3</u>

The Long-Awaited One

The Prophecies

Day 1
Genesis 3:15 &
Genesis 12:1-3

The Messiah was promised from the very beginning.

Genesis 3:15
And I will put enmity
between you and the woman,
and between your offspring and hers;
he will crush your head,
and you will strike his heel."

Genesis 12:1-3
The LORD had said to Abram, "Go from
your country, your people and your father's
household to the land
I will show you.
"I will make you into a great nation,
and I will bless you;
I will make your name great,
and you will be a blessing. I will bless
those who bless you, and whoever curses

you I will curse; and all peoples on earth
will be blessed through you."

It is so much fun to start a new journey, isn't it? There's
the excitement and the planning, but also the nervousness
that stems from the unknown. We are about to embark on a
journey together that leads to what many call the most
wonderful time of the year - Christmas! Much of this journey
is actually very familiar to us. You may be bursting with
anticipation to celebrate again this year. Or just maybe
you're feeling a bit anxious heading into Christmas because
in the past, Christmas has not been a time of quiet reflection
and peace, but a time of frenzied activity and financial stress.
Whatever feelings you are experiencing as you approach this
season, I pray that this year we all take time for some
contemplation on the broader meaning of Christmas. God
sent His only Son into this world to make us right with Him
again. This plan to send Jesus was not some haphazard, last
minute rescue. Instead it is pretty amazing for us to realize
that God's plan for our rescue from sin was in place from the
very beginning.

You see, from the very beginning we needed help.
Created by God to live in communion with Him, we just had
to have our own way and eat from the only tree that was
denied to us. I use the words "we" and "us" and not just
"Adam and Eve" because we all know that we have the same
propensity to believe a lie and pursue our own way. I
guarantee we would all have ended up in the same place that
Adam and Eve did given the chance.

Then as we consider God's reaction to our rebellious
nature, we often focus on the fact that God punished Adam

15

and Eve and forget that even in the curse there was the promise of redemption. The first thing God did in dealing with sin was deal with the serpent who deceived Eve. God went straight to the heart of the problem, the deceiver. And within His words, God sealed Satan's fate by declaring to him that from the seed of a woman, One would come who would crush his head, even though he would strike the heel of the One. Take a moment to let that scene sink in. When we consider how Jesus' story actually unfolded, it looked as though Satan had won when Jesus died on the cross. But God had a bigger plan. Allowing Jesus to take on our punishment and then raising Him back to life to offer us all new life! What a great promise!

Only after God had presented a plan of hope for the future did He deal with the consequences for the woman and the man themselves. Yes, there would now be pain in childbirth and we would have to work very hard for our daily bread. And yes, we would now have to experience death. But, the plan of hope that God set in motion would ultimately deal with the deceptive nature of sin thoroughly and convincingly. *Thank you, Father, for hope even when everything seems hopeless!*

As the story of Genesis continues, we come to our second verse of the day. In Genesis 12, God revealed more of exactly how He would reconnect with us by establishing a people for Himself through Abraham. Then He repeated the promises of a Messiah to each of the leaders of Israel, making it very clear that Messiah would be born through a very specific family line. Continuously God demonstrated His faithfulness by establishing and maintaining them as a people. So that when the time was just right, He would keep the promise He made in the very beginning.

Thank you, Father, that even in dealing with our fall,
You laid out the promise of restoration!

Ephesians 1:3-10

Praise be to the God and Father of our Lord Jesus Christ, who has blessed us in the heavenly realms with every spiritual blessing in Christ. For he chose us in him before the creation of the world to be holy and blameless in his sight. In love he predestined us for adoption to sonship through Jesus Christ, in accordance with his pleasure and will - to the praise of his glorious grace, which he has freely given us in the One he loves. In him we have redemption through his blood, the forgiveness of sins, in accordance with the riches of God's grace that he lavished on us. With all wisdom and understanding, he made known to us the mystery of his will according to his good pleasure, which he purposed in Christ, to be put into effect when the times reach their fulfillment -to bring unity to all things in heaven and on earth under Christ.

The Long-Awaited One

The Prophecies

Day 2
Psalm 118:21-23 &
Isaiah 28:16

The Messiah would be the foundation
of God's plan to redeem us.

Psalm 118:21-23

I will give you thanks,
for you answered me;
you have become my salvation.
The stone the builders rejected has become
the cornerstone;
the Lord has done this,
and it is marvelous in our eyes.

Isaiah 28:16

So this is what the Sovereign LORD says:
"See, I lay a stone in Zion,
a tested stone,
a precious cornerstone for a sure
foundation; the one who relies on it
will never be stricken with panic.

Have you ever been in an old house that had a broken-down foundation? Cracks in the walls, sloping floors, every step met with a creaking noise. It can feel rather scary. My husband and I toured a house or two like this during a home search. It was truly unsettling just walking through these houses. We certainly couldn't envision ourselves living in a house where we worried if the very floors beneath us would support us. A strong, solid foundation is absolutely critical. If the foundation is not built correctly, the house will not stand the test of time.

In today's passages, God is drawing upon the powerful visual of the foundation to help us realize just how vital the role of the Messiah would be. In the construction of the masonry on a building, the cornerstone or foundation stone is the first stone set in place. Its position is critical since all the other stones will be placed in reference to this stone, determining the stability of the entire structure.

This is the role God has chosen for the Messiah. The Messiah would be the very foundation of God's plan to restore His creation. Everything God would do to redeem His people would be based on what He would do through Jesus. The entire narrative of the Old Testament would build and ultimately be completed in Jesus, the Messiah.

For those of us on this side of history, it is much easier to recognize the way God laid the groundwork for Jesus' coming and for the work He would do for us by submitting to death on the cross and rising again. We can see the whole picture of all God accomplished for us through Jesus. We see the references to grace and mercy as God worked with His people. We can see how Jesus fulfilled prophecy after prophecy, demonstrating how He is the foundation of God's plan for redemption.

For the people of Jesus' time, however, it was not so easy to see. Many people of that era had preconceived ideas of how they thought God would bring about the redemption of His people. Many envisioned God sending them another earthly king just like King David, a great king who would defeat their enemies and bring back the glory days of the nation of Israel. So, it was hard for them to accept as Messiah a baby born in a stable to a poor family whose marriage came together in a rather questionable fashion. So much of Jesus' life and ministry did not fit their vision of how God would work. Certainly, dying on a cross did not fit their idea of what God would plan. So, for many of the Israelites, Jesus was "the stone the builders rejected." In their minds, this could not possibly be God's plan.

Their unbelief did not halt God's plans, however. Aren't we glad that we serve a God whose plans do not revolve around our understanding of everything He is doing as He is doing it? We gain a sense of assurance as God faithfully continues to set His great plan in motion even as He patiently waits for us to recognize His plan for what it is - our very lifeline!

Thank You, Father, for continuously setting Your will in motion, even as we struggle to fully understand. Thank You that as we look back on what You did through Jesus, we gain confidence that, if You could so skillfully and masterfully pull together such a marvelous plan, You will continue to work through us every day in every circumstance. We are so grateful for Your provision for us through Jesus!

The Long-Awaited One

The Prophecies

Day 3
Isaiah 11:1-5, 10 &
Isaiah 16:5

The Messiah would be our righteous judge.

Isaiah 16:5

In love a throne will be established;
in faithfulness a man will sit on it –
one from the house of David –
one who in judging seeks justice and
speeds the cause of righteousness.

Isaiah 11:1-5, 10

A shoot will come up from
the stump of Jesse;
from his roots a Branch will bear fruit. The
Spirit of the LORD will rest on him - the
Spirit of wisdom and of understanding,
the Spirit of counsel and of might,
the Spirit of the knowledge
and fear of the LORD –
and he will delight in the fear

of the LORD.
He will not judge by what he sees
with his eyes,
or decide by what he hears
with his ears;
but with righteousness he will judge
the needy,
justice he will give decisions for the poor
of the earth.
He will strike the earth with
the rod of his mouth;
the breath of his lips he will
slay the wicked.
Righteousness will be his belt and
faithfulness the sash around his waist.

In that day the Root of Jesse will stand as a
banner for the peoples; the nations will
rally to him, and his resting place will be
glorious.

Picture this - Your television screen goes black and the
words "Law & Order" come on the screen. Then you hear a
voice saying,

"In the criminal justice system, the people are
represented by two separate but equally important

groups: the police, who investigate crime, and the district attorneys, who prosecute the offenders. These are their stories. DUN DUN"

I have always loved criminal justice shows. It's so gratifying to see criminals being brought to justice. Of course, there are the episodes in which the criminal gets away with it and we feel so angry. A deep need for justice is built into our conscience. It is one of our greatest needs. Knowing that if someone wrongs us, they will be held accountable. And we want that justice to be swift and fair. No doubt, as soon as I said we all need justice, a situation came to mind when you needed a fair, honest judgement. You or your family were wronged. You needed an advocate. And too often in this world, justice seems to favor the ones who have enough money or influence in the community to get their own way. The big insurance company prevails over the little guy with a chronic disease. The husband who left his family now refuses to pay the child support. The drunk driver who, because she knows the right people, never serves a day in jail while you are left grieving. The list goes on and on. Injustice can crush our souls and rob us of hope.

That's why this picture of Messiah as our righteous judge who "speeds the cause of the righteous" and "gives decisions for the poor of the earth," is so vital to us all! Messiah will be the King who stands "as a banner for the peoples" and judges with wisdom and understanding. What an incredible promise!

It was this very promise that helped me heal after watching my brother receive no real justice as he brought his abuser before the courts. The man who hurt him, even though he was found guilty after admitting his crimes, was never punished for those offenses because of his position in the community. The injustice cut deep, but I didn't have to seek revenge to make things right. I didn't have to hold on to my anger and resentment at the preferential treatment given to the offender. Instead, I could rest in the knowledge that ultimately God would judge; and God would make things right. That allowed me to slowly forgive and even begin to pray for the offender.

Thank you, Father, that Your Spirit will bring

righteous judgement, peace, and even forgiveness!

The Long-Awaited One

Day 4
Psalm 110:1-4

Messiah will be our priest forever, seated at
God's right hand.

Psalm 110:1-4
The LORD says to my lord:
"Sit at my right hand until I make your
enemies a footstool for your feet."
The LORD will extend your mighty
scepter from Zion, saying,
"Rule in the midst of your enemies!" Your
troops will be willing on your
day of battle.
Arrayed in holy splendor,
your young men will come to you like dew
from the morning's womb.
The LORD has sworn and will not change
his mind:
"You are a priest forever,
in the order of Melchizedek."

Have you ever met a celebrity or someone whose work you have always admired but never thought you would get the chance to meet in person? It's nerve-racking, isn't it? Your mind starts to spin with questions. Do I look all right? What do I say? Is it ok to tell them what a huge fan I am of their work? Do I sound like a strange groupie?

One of my favorite demonstrations of this is "Mr. Bean meets the Queen of England." In his usual awkward fashion, we see Mr. Bean waiting in line to meet the Queen. As he waits, he practices his handshake and his bow. He checks his breath and his shoes and clothes. He even manages to floss his teeth with another person's loose thread. All his efforts are in vain, however. When it comes to his turn, he finally gets himself composed only to knock the Queen to the floor with his overly enthusiastic bow. The poor man! His best efforts fall short in the face of royalty.

Do you ever feel like that before God? He's our Creator. He created the entire universe in all its complexity, setting the very laws of science in motion. So holy and pure and beyond all we can imagine. In the face of His righteousness, we are confronted with just how unworthy we are to even consider being in His presence. Standing in His presence seems so far out of our reach. If we read about the first places of worship God prescribed, we realize that people were not allowed to enter God's presence casually. They needed a priest to step between them and God. There was even a place where God's presence would dwell called the Holy of Holies and only one select priest a year could enter through the veil. Wow! God certainly went to a lot of trouble to establish that His holiness was not to be taken lightly and that because of our sin, we were now separated from Him and needed a priest to intercede for us.

In today's verse, God tells us that the Messiah would sit at God's right hand and be our priest forever. That means that if you are a follower of Christ, you now have an advocate interceding for you all the time! How powerful is that? And because you do, you can now enter God's presence with confidence, knowing Jesus has completed the work on your behalf and made you right with God. How amazing is that? Now we can approach God with freedom and assurance because of the work of the cross. God demonstrated that His presence was now accessible to us as He tore the temple veil in two from top to bottom when Jesus died. (Matthew 27:50-51) Because of Jesus, the barrier between God and us was now removed. Of course, we don't enter His presence flippantly but with a sense of awe and wonder that the God of the universe went to such great lengths to draw us to Himself.

Thank you, Father, that what Jesus did on our behalf took care of our sins – past, present, and future.

Take a little time to remember what an awesome gift it is that we can now enter God's presence so freely. Knowing that even when our words fail us, we have the gift of Jesus acting as our priest and interceding on our behalf.

Hebrews 4:14-16

Therefore, since we have a great high priest who has ascended into heaven, Jesus the Son of God, let us hold firmly to the faith we profess. For we do not have a high priest who is unable to empathize with our weaknesses, but we have one who has been tempted in every way, just as we are - yet he did not sin. Let us then approach God's throne of grace with confidence, so that we may receive mercy and find grace to help us in our time of need.

The Long-Awaited One

The Prophecies

Day 5
Isaiah 9:2, 6-7

The names given to the Promised One.

Isaiah 9:2, 6-7

The people walking in darkness
have seen a great light;
on those living in the land of deep
darkness a light has dawned.
For to us a child is born,
to us a son is given,
and the government will be
on his shoulders.
And he will be called
Wonderful Counselor, Mighty God,
Everlasting Father, Prince of Peace.
Of the greatness of his government and
peace there will be no end.
He will reign on David's throne and
over his kingdom,
establishing and upholding it
with justice and righteousness
from that time on and forever.

The zeal of the LORD Almighty
will accomplish this.

As a child, I really didn't like my name. The only people I ever met who had the name Pauline were old women. Why couldn't my parents have given me a cooler name? My mom enjoyed telling me the story of how my dad loved that name and she agreed to use the name if she could find a middle name that complimented it. She found one, and I was given the name Pauline Michelle. It did help knowing that my name was chosen lovingly by my parents, but I still wasn't crazy about it. The longer I was in school though, the more I realized it was nice having a rather unique name. When I heard someone yell, "Pauline," I could be fairly certain they were calling for me. And as I was growing up, I never once needed a last initial attached to my name to differentiate me from another Pauline in the room. I grew to appreciate the uniqueness of my name. There is power in a name.

Throughout the Bible, God reveals Himself to His people using His many names which declare His nature. This is something that is lost in many modern translations of the Bible but is highly significant. For instance, one of God's names, Jehovah or Yahweh means "I am" revealing the truth that God always was and always will be. Another name, El Shaddai, tells us that God is Almighty. The name El Roi means He is the God who sees all. The name Adonai tells us God is Lord over all. We can learn so much about God and His character through His names.

So, it should not surprise us in today's passage that the writer, when telling us about the coming Messiah, would use a list of names to reveal Messiah's character. Let's just take a few minutes and examine the meanings of the names we're given in today's verse.

Wonderful – Messiah would be unique among mankind, and the glory of who He is and what He has done should fill us with absolute awe and wonder.

Counselor – Messiah would speak the very wisdom of God, revealing the mind and heart of God.

Mighty God – Messiah was fully human and yet fully divine. He is God Almighty.

Everlasting Father – Another translation of this would be "Father of Eternity," the source or author of all eternity.

Prince of Peace – Messiah would be the One who would bring peace between God and man.

There is so much truth and hope packed in the names of Messiah!

Jesus Messiah, You are the source of absolute wonder and awe as we take in who You are. You are the source of all wisdom and understanding. You are God wrapped in human flesh and living among us, Immanuel. You are the source of all time and space. And You are the source of light, hope and peace in this dark, broken world. We praise Your name!

31

Days 6-7 What we learn about Messiah's birth....

Days 8-9 What we learn about Messiah's life...

The Long-Awaited One

The Prophecies
His Birth

Day 6
Isaiah 7:14

Messiah would be born of a virgin and called Immanuel.

Isaiah 7:14

Therefore the Lord himself will give you a
sign: The virgin will conceive and give
birth to a son and will call him Immanuel.

Do you struggle to surrender your warm, comfortable life to go serve someone? I know I do. When I was younger, I thought nothing of heading off to the poorest region of the island of Jamaica and sleeping on a cot in a non-air-conditioned dorm room. We spent our days sanding and digging while working alongside our Jamaican friends building a medical clinic under the bright Caribbean sun. Then there were the summers I spent as a camp counselor sleeping in open-ended covered wagons for weeks on end. Yes, you read that correctly; we slept in covered wagons at the camp. They were pretty cool. Apparently, the bugs and critters thought so too, because they entered the wagons

34

regularly! I was young and adventurous though, so no problem. Now that I'm a bit older, I'm not sure I would sign up for these conditions again without some serious prayer!

Let's face it, we love our comfort. It gets harder every year to want to camp in a tent when I could stay in a lovely bed and breakfast just about anywhere and sleep in luxury, awakening to breakfast already prepared. As lovely as my favorite comforts are in this temporary world, imagine what Jesus relinquished to come to live among us. Unthinkable, isn't it? He left behind the glory of heaven to be Immanuel, God with us. He came and lived an ordinary life as a man, so that he would experience our struggles and temptations first-hand. Incredibly, He came willingly. What an amazing God we serve!

We also learn in today's passage that Messiah's birth was set-apart and special. Born in the ordinary way to a woman but born of a virgin so we would know His Father was not a mere man. It was a quiet, gentle entrance to this earth and yet His conception defied the very laws of nature. Leave it to God to display His incredible power in such a quiet, yet supernatural way.

Thank You, Father, for entering this world in such a quiet, yet powerful way. And thank You for living among us and bringing us back to You, so that someday we could know the incomparable comforts of heaven.

The Long-Awaited One

The Prophecies
His Birth

Day 7
Micah 5:2-5a

The Messiah would be born in Bethlehem.

Micah 5:2-5a

"But you, Bethlehem Ephrathah,
though you are small among the
clans of Judah,
out of you will come for me
one who will be ruler over Israel,
whose origins are from of old,
from ancient times."
Therefore, Israel will be abandoned
until the time when she who is in labor
bears a son,
and the rest of his brothers return
to join the Israelites.
He will stand and shepherd his flock
in the strength of the LORD,
in the majesty of the name of the
LORD his God.

And they will live securely,
for then his greatness will reach to the
ends of the earth.
And he will be our peace.

"You will spend your old age in prosperity and peace." These were the words printed on the slip of paper in my fortune cookie at lunch one day after church. I saved them because I liked them. I mean, who doesn't want to spend their old age in prosperity and peace? Of course, I realize it's just a fortune cookie, and it holds no power to make anything actually happen in my life; but we all have a desire to know things will work out in the end. People are often fascinated by fortune-tellers and horoscopes because we want the assurance that everything is going to come together for our good. We want to know we will live our "happily ever after." Ultimately, however, we realize that a slip of paper with some nice words or a column predicting our future based on the day of our birth holds no real power.

In today's passage, we see God foretelling the future in a rather detailed way to help His people clearly recognize the Messiah. The Messiah would be born of a woman in the town of Bethlehem. God gets very specific and probably causes a few jaws to drop as He tells His people that the Messiah would be born in a rather insignificant little town. If you ever wonder if God can do something great through something seemingly insignificant, remember He sent Jesus into the world as a tiny infant, born in a tiny town. Then He worked through those humble beginnings to work out our salvation. God can do anything and use any situation!

God can devise an incredibly detailed, elaborate plan over hundreds of years through many people, and bring each detail to fruition. Over the next few days and weeks, we will read about the amazing details God revealed about the coming Messiah. As we read detail after detail that God designed and then fulfilled, may it strengthen our faith and trust that ultimately God will do everything that He promises to do. And the Messiah will be all that God promises He will be. In today's passage, we're promised a strong, majestic Shepherd who will be our peace. I pray that your Christmas is filled with His peace and the assurance that God's plan is always for our good.

Romans 8:28-30

"**And we know that in all things God works for the good of those who love him, who[a] have been called according to his purpose. For those God foreknew he also predestined to be conformed to the image of his Son, that he might be the firstborn among many brothers and sisters. And those he predestined, he also called; those he called, he also justified; those he justified, he also glorified.**"

The Long-Awaited One

Day 8
Isaiah 61:1-3

What Messiah's life would look like.

Isaiah 61:1-3

The Spirit of the Sovereign LORD
is on me,
because the LORD has anointed me
to proclaim good news to the poor.
He has sent me to bind up the
brokenhearted,
to proclaim freedom for the captives and
release from darkness
for the prisoners,
to proclaim the year of
the LORD's favor
and the day of vengeance of our God, to
comfort all who mourn,
and provide for those who grieve
in Zion –

to bestow on them a crown of beauty
instead of ashes,
the oil of joy
instead of mourning,
and a garment of praise
instead of a spirit of despair.
They will be called oaks of righteousness,
a planting of the LORD
for the display of his splendor.

Today's picture of the Messiah is particularly interesting because it is the passage that Jesus chose to read when He entered the synagogue in Nazareth, his hometown. In Luke 4:16-21, we are told that "Jesus went to Nazareth, where He had been brought up." As usual, on the Sabbath He went into the synagogue and began to read from the scrolls. He read the first verse of the passage we just read. Then He sat down and declared that, "Today this scripture is fulfilled in your hearing." What a powerful statement! He was proclaiming Himself to be the Messiah! His listeners would not have missed that concept as He read these words. Needless to say, His words were met with immediate skepticism; and once the people in the synagogue confronted Him, they ended up driving Him out of town.

The people of Jesus' hometown could not see just how true Jesus' declaration was. They saw a young man who they had watched grow up. How could He be the promised one of God? They could not see Him for what God declared Him to be, Messiah. I wonder how many of us miss who Jesus truly is because of our excuses or a limited view. Do we inhibit

God and all that He could do in our lives because we only see the short-term and not the big picture? Do we trust Him at His word?

If we read the complete passage, we notice a description of the work Jesus did to fulfill the Scripture every day of His three-year ministry. He did proclaim freedom. He did proclaim God's favor and God's wrath. He did comfort those who mourn. He did provide for the grieving. For three years Jesus was a walking picture of this passage as He traveled preaching and teaching, healing and comforting. Because we get the benefit of looking backwards at completed events, it all appears very clear to us. Jesus did exactly what this passage says He would do. May we never doubt it, but instead gain new confidence that Jesus truly is the fulfillment of all that God promised. And those promises are for us today. May we know that God sent His Son to fulfill for us the beautiful promise found in verse three.

Messiah would, "bestow on them a crown of beauty instead of ashes, the oil of joy instead of mourning, And a garment of praise instead of a spirit of despair."

Thank You, Father, for showing the world ahead of time just what Messiah would do as He was on the earth living among us. We praise You, Lord, that through Jesus we have hope that You can bring beauty and joy into our lives where there was ugliness and despair.

The Long-Awaited One

The Prophecies
His Life

Day 9
Psalm 118:26-28 &
Zechariah 9:9

Palm Sunday is foretold.

Psalm 118:26-28

Blessed is he who comes in the name of
the LORD.
From the house of the LORD
we bless you.
The LORD is God,
and he has made his light shine on us.
With boughs in hand, join in
the festal procession
up to the horns of the altar.
You are my God, and I will praise you; you
are my God, and I will exalt you.

Zechariah 9:9

Rejoice greatly, Daughter Zion!
Shout, Daughter Jerusalem!
See, your king comes to you,
righteous and victorious,
lowly and riding on a donkey,
on a colt, the foal of a donkey.

Such an awesome set of passages describing a specific event in the life of Jesus which is documented in all four of the gospel accounts of Jesus' life (Matthew 21; Mark 11; Luke 19; John 12). So, the eyewitnesses to the events thought it was an important event to share. In the prophetic view of the day, we see that the Messiah would come to them "lowly and riding on a donkey." They would have "boughs in hand" as they "join in the festal procession" singing the praises of their King. Even the words they spoke, "Blessed is He who comes in the name of the Lord," were foretold. So much detail was given hundreds of years in advance!

You would think this would help the Jewish people fully recognize Jesus as the Messiah. The events of the day indicate they did recognize Him, even if for only a day. But it didn't take long for them to switch from shouting His praises, "Blessed is He who comes in the name of the Lord," to screaming "Crucify Him!" In just a few days they fell away when Jesus didn't behave the way they thought He should if He was truly the Messiah. Sometimes I think, "how could they miss it? God was so clear." But I know that in my own heart and mind, I often miss the mark as well. It is far too easy for me to doubt and worry and question.

Oh, that I would trust His plan even when it becomes unclear. Oh, that I would trust His character when circumstances make me doubt His goodness. Oh, that I would trust His power when the events around me seem overwhelming. Oh, that I would trust that He sees all when my little corner of the world seems hidden from His view. Oh, that I would trust that ultimately, He will win even when it seems that evil is taking over the entire world. And in learning to trust, may I learn to shout His praises and share all that He has done for me. And when fear and worry creep in again, may I remember His faithfulness and grow in my faith in Him.

Days 10-15 What we learn about Messiah's Death....

The Long-Awaited One

The Prophecies
His Death

Day 10
Psalm 41:9 &
Zechariah 11:12-13, 13:7

The Messiah would be betrayed and abandoned.

Psalm 41:9
Even my close friend, someone I trusted,
one who shared my bread,
has turned against me.

Zechariah 11:12-13
I told them, "If you think it best, give me
my pay; but if not, keep it." So, they paid
me thirty pieces of silver.
And the LORD said to me, "Throw it to
the potter" -the handsome price at which
they valued me! So, I took the thirty pieces
of silver and threw them to the potter at
the house of the LORD.

Zechariah 13:7

"Awake, sword, against my shepherd,
against the man who is close to me!"
declares the LORD Almighty.
"Strike the shepherd,
and the sheep will be scattered,
and I will turn my hand
against the little ones."

Do you ever feel like the whole world is against you? Even those closest to you? You've been betrayed by a coworker, passed over for yet another promotion, deeply hurt by a friend, unappreciated by your spouse, or maybe you just feel forgotten and unloved. We have all been there.

Jesus knew this feeling well. He had spent three years traveling with twelve men as His closest companions. There were so many highs and lows as they traveled teaching, healing, raising the dead, and dealing with the Jewish leaders. It was quite a ride with moments of brilliant success and moments of fear as they escaped the many plots to harm Jesus. Crowds followed Him everywhere and gathered wherever He made an appearance. There were even more people who followed Jesus and the twelve, listening to Jesus and helping to meet the many needs that came with a traveling ministry. It was an exciting time.

Ministry like that would have really drawn Jesus and His closest followers together. So, it's hard to imagine them abandoning Him, but that's exactly what happened when Jesus needed them the most. The craziest part is Jesus knew they would. Could you calmly tell your betrayers that you knew exactly what they were about to do? And yet, that's what He does with Judas, Peter, and the rest of the disciples in the garden. Even facing what was to come, the crucifixion, Jesus looked them in the eye and revealed to them that He knew what was about to take place.

Not only was He aware of what they would do, He was ready to forgive and restore them to ministry after they had deserted Him. That's a level of forgiveness I cannot wrap my head around. Apparently, Judas could not understand either. He took his own life when he realized that he could not undo his betrayal. The others simply ran for cover. The bravest one, Peter, stayed close by during the night of the arrest only to find himself disowning Jesus, just as Jesus had told him he would. Can you imagine the despair they must have felt as they watched Jesus die wondering if they would be next?

Jesus was left to face the worst death imaginable alone. Talk about betrayal and abandonment. And yet, after Jesus was raised back to life, He chose these very men who had abandoned Him, to carry the news of all that He had said and done throughout the world. Now that's forgiveness! They could truly teach the message of salvation and restoration found in the hope of Jesus because they had experienced it first-hand!

Now we too can say with confidence that our Messiah truly does know our sufferings, physical and relational. We can trust that He knows our hearts and is always ready to forgive and restore and heal. May we always remember that, "the one who calls us is faithful and He will do it" (1 Thess. 5:24). May our hearts be strengthened to love Him more deeply and may we all boldly proclaim all that He has done for us.

The Long-Awaited One

The Prophecies
His Death

Day 11
Psalm 22:1, 7-8, 16-18

A very specific portrait of Messiah's death.

Psalm 22:1, 7-8, 16-18

My God, my God, why have you forsaken
me?
Why are you so far from saving me,
so far from my cries of anguish?

All who see me mock me;
they hurl insults, shaking their heads. "He
trusts in the LORD," they say,
"let the LORD rescue him. Let him deliver
him, since he delights in him."

Dogs surround me,
a pack of villains encircles me;
they pierce[a] my hands and my feet.
All my bones are on display;
people stare and gloat over me.

They divide my clothes among them and
cast lots for my garments.

This passage is one of those that always blows my mind with the details it includes. This is a Psalm of David, who is known for pouring out His heart to God, often with startling boldness and honesty. Many of the psalms of David include deep heart cries calling on God's power to help him receive justice against his many enemies. David had been promised by God that he would be the next king of Israel, but it took years for that to come to pass. And in those years of waiting, he spent a lot of time on the run, not an easy path to the throne. But in this heart cry, God takes David to a new place in his expression. David becomes a prophet.

I often wonder if David was actually given mental pictures of what he was prophesying. Could he see the Messiah suffering on the cross? You would almost think so considering the detailed description, but we don't know for sure. We do know that the details are incredibly descriptive of exactly how Jesus died, despite the fact that Roman crucifixion wasn't even developed for another 1,000 years. That's pretty amazing!

Believe it or not, there are people who take the time to try to refute the prophecies of the Messiah. One of the arguments against Jesus fulfilling the prophecies is called intentional fulfillment. This argument states that Jesus learned all the prophecies and went around purposely fulfilling them. There are certainly a few of the prophecies Jesus could have fulfilled deliberately. However, He had no control over details like His birthplace. The events of the crucifixion are another strong example that refute this argument. Jesus had no control over His accusers or the guards who arrested Him. He could not influence the crowd who asked for Barabbas or the soldiers who gambled for His clothes. Nor could He control the fact that the soldiers would not break His bones to speed His death but instead would pierce His side. Details like these show that God had set forth a plan that no mere man could perfectly fulfill without His direction and supernatural oversight. God's plan for our redemption was incredibly detailed and thorough in its scope. Who else but our God would do so much and go so far to make sure you and I could be made whole?

Thank You, Father God, for setting forth and orchestrating a beautifully detailed plan that allows for us to know You and to be known by You, a plan that makes us whole and makes us Your children. What amazing promises!

The Long-Awaited One

The Prophecies
His Death

Day 12
Exodus 12:3, 5-7, 12-14, 46

Messiah would be the embodiment of the Passover Lamb.

Exodus 12:3, 5-7, 12-14, 46

Tell the whole community of Israel that
on the tenth day of this month each man is
to take a lamb for his family,
one for each household.

The animals you choose must be year-old
males without defect, and you may take
them from the sheep or the goats. Take care
of them until the fourteenth day of the
month, when all the members of the
community of Israel must slaughter them at
twilight. Then they are to take some of the
blood and put it on the sides and tops of the
doorframes of the houses where they eat
the lambs.

"On that same night I will pass through
Egypt and strike down every firstborn of
both people and animals, and I will bring
judgment on all the gods of Egypt. I am the
LORD. The blood will be a sign for you on
the houses where you are, and when I see
the blood, I will pass over you. No
destructive plague will touch you when I
strike Egypt.
This is a day you are to commemorate; for
the generations to come you shall celebrate
it as a festival to the Lord – a lasting
ordinance.

"It must be eaten inside the house; take
none of the meat outside the house. Do not
break any of the bones."

One of the most incredible things about the way God
reveals Himself to us is the way He continually uses
foreshadowing. He would often work in the lives of His
people, the Israelites, in ways that mimicked what He would
do later through Jesus. One of the strongest examples of this
is when God set His people free from Egypt through the
Passover.

The Passover was a specific time set aside by God's
command to remember what God did for His people, Israel,
to liberate them from slavery in Egypt. The passage you read

today from the book of Exodus was the specific instructions from God for His people as they prepared for one of God's biggest miracles. It must have seemed at least a little bit odd to be painting their doorframes in blood before eating unleavened bread and bitter herbs. They must have been wondering exactly what God had in store. Yet, they knew not to question since they had just watched God send down nine plagues against Egypt in an effort to move Pharaoh to release His people. But this last plague was special. Maybe they thought God was being cruel when they learned that He planned to kill the first-born sons of the Egyptians. Maybe you think it was cruel punishment but remember God had already given Pharaoh multiple chances but to no avail. He didn't start with a death sentence; Pharaoh's hard heart left room for nothing else. Whatever their feelings must have been, they realized God meant business, and it was time to follow the plan He set forth. By following God's plan and using the blood of the sacrificial lamb, God's people were spared and then set free.

Fast forward to the time of Jesus. We see Jesus gathering with His disciples to celebrate the Passover together in Jerusalem. They were remembering God's faithfulness in the past as they sat down to that table, but Jesus was going to show them that the events of the past had a deeper significance for their time. For days, He had been talking to them about the time reaching its fulfillment when He would have to leave them, but they couldn't understand what He meant. They were even more confused when He took the bread and the cup at dinner and told them that the elements would symbolize what He was about to do. His body broken for them? His blood shed for them? What could He mean? They could not understand until after it all came to pass. Then looking back on Jesus' death, burial, and resurrection, it became clear as they recalled all that He had said and done. Jesus, through His death on the cross, became the ultimate sacrificial Lamb.

He was the embodiment of what God said the Passover Lamb should be, without stain or blemish – sinless, and His blood was shed to cover us from God's wrath. And just to drive home the point even more, there was the detail that none of His bones would be broken. (Another detail Jesus could not make happen, as we discussed in yesterday's devotional reading.) What an awesome God we serve! So perfectly coordinated that He laid out a plan that would at one time set His people free from tyranny in Egypt while it perfectly foreshadowed His ultimate plan to set all people free from sin and death through Jesus, the Lamb of God.

Thank You, Father, for the gift of our sacrificial Lamb, Jesus. Thank You that on the cross, He wiped away the need to constantly make sacrifices to atone for our sins. We praise You, Jesus, for bearing the weight of our sins, taking them upon Yourself, and setting us free from the punishment we deserved. Thank You, God!

The Long-Awaited One

The Prophecies
His Death

Day 13
Isaiah 52:13-15

The Messiah would suffer on our behalf.

Isaiah 52:13-15

See, my servant will act wisely;
he will be raised and lifted up
and highly exalted.
Just as there were many who were
appalled at him –
his appearance was so disfigured beyond
that of any human being and his form
marred beyond human likeness - so he will
sprinkle many nations,
and kings will shut their mouths because
of him.
For what they were not told,
they will see,
and what they have not heard,
they will understand.

This passage leads to one of the greatest prophetic passages in the entire Old Testament, but that's for another day. Here Isaiah tells us exactly how Jesus would become our true Passover Lamb. Jesus would suffer beyond what we can imagine to sprinkle us with His blood and make us clean. He suffered so greatly that He was completely disfigured. Have you ever seen someone after a traumatic injury when the swelling and bruising is so severe that they were unrecognizable? It's pretty awful to see. But this was the level of suffering Jesus endured for us.

There have been people who have studied the effects of death by crucifixion, and it is believed to be the cruelest form of punishment ever invented. Every system of the body was slowly and painfully shut down. There were many prisoners who did not survive even the beating that led up to being placed on the cross. It was not for the faint of heart.

Take a minute to let that sink in. Jesus suffered horrifically on your behalf. I don't know how He endured the worst possible punishment when it was completely undeserved. But He did, and He did it for you and for me. Wow!

In the midst of the description of His suffering, Isaiah says that Messiah would "sprinkle many nations. "By spilling His blood, Jesus once again takes on a priestly role. When the priests of the old covenant would offer sacrifices for sin, there was a time when they would sprinkle the people with the blood as a picture of how the blood covered them, making them right with God. This is what Jesus did for us by becoming the sacrifice for our sins. His sacrifice paid the penalty for our sins, and His blood washes us as white as snow. What a Savior!

Romans 5:6-8

"You see, at just the right time, when we were still powerless, Christ died for the ungodly. Very rarely will anyone die for a righteous person, though for a good person someone might possibly dare to die. But God demonstrates His own love for us in this: While we were still sinners, Christ died for us."

The Long-Awaited One

The Prophecies
His Death

Day 14
Zechariah 12:10-13:1

Messiah's death would be for cleansing.

Zechariah 12:10-13:1

"And I will pour out on the house of David and the inhabitants of Jerusalem a spirit of grace and supplication. They will look on me, the one they have pierced, and they will mourn for him as one mourns for an only child, and grieve bitterly for him as one grieves for a firstborn son. On that day the weeping in Jerusalem will be as great as the weeping of Hadad Rimmon in the plain of Megiddo. The land will mourn, each clan by itself, with their wives by themselves: the clan of the house of David and their wives, the clan of the house of Nathan and their wives, the clan of the house of Levi and their wives, the clan of Shimei and

their wives, and all the rest of the clans and
their wives.
"On that day a fountain will be opened to
the house of David and the inhabitants of
Jerusalem, to cleanse them from sin and
impurity.

Once again, we're reminded that Jesus came "to cleanse us from sin and impurity." What a precious gift! The greatest gift we will ever receive - grace! Obviously, Jesus coming to die for us and making us right with God was the central focus of why Jesus came. God was very clear as He informed us that the primary objective of Jesus' mission was to reconcile us with the Father through Jesus' blood.

But there is a sad side to this story. We're told that the Jewish people would see their Messiah, "the one they have pierced," and they would weep and mourn. Oh, the sadness of regret. What had they done?

Looking back at the events that led up to Jesus' crucifixion, I can't imagine the frenzied activity of the Passover week. The huge crowds as people gathered to celebrate the Passover. The stories people were inevitably sharing regarding this man Jesus who had been causing quite a stir for the past three years. The rejoicing as Jesus entered Jerusalem on a donkey as they proclaimed Him the Messiah. But then, when things didn't go as they expected, the leaders were able to incite the crowd into a crazed mob that demanded Jesus' death.

How did things change so quickly? What were they thinking? I'm always asking myself that question when I look at these days in the life of Jesus. I wonder how I would have reacted. Studies show that the mob mentality overrides thought and reason. So, unless I'm ever in that situation, I'll never fully understand. But let's take a few moments to envision being there in Jerusalem on this crazy emotional roller coaster, trying to understand all that we are seeing and hearing, being confronted with the ugly reality of watching Jesus being beaten, bruised, pierced and then dying on the cross. Just imagine the many questions that would run rampant through your mind.

There were many reactions among the people. Some stayed angry and mocked Jesus while others scattered and hid. Still others were seen weeping at the foot of the cross. Their dream of what Messiah would be was nailed to a cross, and they mourned. A number of them got stuck in their mourning and never sought the truth of who Jesus truly was and what He came to do. But some followers stayed close and gathered as a community to see what God would do next. And for the final group, there was joy as they saw Jesus alive again after the resurrection. But that is a story for another day!

Today we need to ask ourselves, are we truly seeking God and allowing Him to fully reveal Himself as He really is, or are we letting our own perceptions of who we think God is cloud our trust in Him? Do we follow our agenda or His? Do we see Him as Scripture reveals or as we would have Him be? Do we trust that His plan is bigger than the temporary situations in which we find ourselves?

The Long-Awaited One

The Prophecies
His Death

Day 15
Matthew 12:38-40

Messiah relates the sign of Jonah to what He would suffer.

Matthew 12:38-40

Then some of the Pharisees and teachers of
the law said to him, "Teacher, we want to
see a sign from you."
He answered, "A wicked and adulterous
generation asks for a sign! But none will be
given it except the sign of the prophet
Jonah. For as Jonah was three days and
three nights in the belly of a huge fish, so
the Son of Man will be three days and three
nights in the heart of the earth.

"Hindsight is 20/20." Some of the truest words ever
spoken. Just thinking about the phrase brings situations to
our minds which demonstrate this perfectly. Stuck in the
middle of the events surrounding us, we can't understand

just what is happening or how to deal with things. Yet somehow, we muddle through; and with time and growing wisdom and experience we look back on those times and we recognize God's hand at work in the midst of our lives. Everything is clarified on the other side of our emotions, worries, fears, and doubts. It's also true as we recall our mistakes. Let's face it, as parents, it's what makes us nervous when our children start making their own decisions. Because of experience, we see clearly what pitfalls they need to avoid, and it scares us to think they may make mistakes that they will suffer the consequences for their entire lives. As young people, you see the fun parents are denying you. While your parents see the future regret bad choices can cause. Hindsight...

When we read the gospels, we see Jesus warn His disciples in several places that He would have to die and be raised again, but they couldn't understand what He meant. And before we get too critical of them, how could they imagine that Jesus meant His death on a cross and His rising from the dead? Those were certainly not everyday occurrences!

In today's passage, we find Jesus being confronted by some of the scribes and Pharisees. They were demanding a sign from Jesus to prove He was the Messiah. Wow! The audacity of demanding signs when they had seen and heard so much already. These men were really struggling through an internal war between the obvious and what they wanted to be true. Jesus replies brilliantly as usual by explaining to them that they have already been given a sign in the life of Jonah. "As Jonah was three days and three nights in the belly of a huge fish, so the Son of Man will be three days and three nights in the heart of the earth." Jesus is using Jonah's story to foreshadow what was about to happen to Him so that on the other side of the swirling, hectic events, people could remember His words and realize it was all part of the plan. He was also drawing these scholars' attention to the fact that God had been continuously revealing His plan all throughout history, whether in direct predictions or in types, which is just a way saying that God worked in people's lives in the Old Testament in ways that would mirror the work He was going to do through Jesus. What an amazing God, and what an amazing plan!

Are you as thankful as I am that we live at this time in history? We can look back on the completed work of Jesus with 20/20 vision. We can now see clearly how God's plan came together in perfect timing as we read eye-witness accounts about how Jesus came and finished the work He was given to do as the Messiah. How awesome is that?

If only I was better at remembering that in my everyday life! I must get better at remembering that I serve a God who is infinitely detailed and perfect in His plans. If I did, I could learn to trust Him even more. I would remember that His plans are best, and He will use everything from my pain and my failures to my triumphs for His ultimate glory. Then, I would live with a new sense of purpose and patience to persevere even when the way sometimes seems unclear. I would remember that He is in control and His ways are much better than mine. And my life is not my own, but a part of something much greater than me.

Thank you, Father, for being a patient God who lovingly moves us along, drawing us to Yourself day after day as You work all things together to complete Your good and perfect will. It is so wonderful to know our lives are in Your hands!

Days 16 - 18 What we learn about Messiah's resurrection....

The Long-Awaited One

The Prophecies
His Resurrection

Day 16
Psalm 16:8-11

The Messiah would not see decay.

Psalm 16:8-11

I keep my eyes always on the LORD. With
him at my right hand,
I will not be shaken.
Therefore my heart is glad and my tongue
rejoices;
my body also will rest secure,
because you will not abandon me to the
realm of the dead,
nor will you let your faithful one
see decay.
You make known to me the path of life;
you will fill me with joy in your presence,
with eternal pleasures at your right hand.

Redemption... Power over death... What precious promises! Our hope lies in these beautiful, poetic words. God would not let His holy One see decay. Instead, Jesus would be risen from the dead! Hallelujah! And now we're promised that through Jesus we too have the hope of eternal life. Thank You, Father! We rejoice in that promise, but in this world, death is still a very real part of our lives.

In the last year and a half, I've lost two people who were significant in my life. First, I lost my brother. There are no words to describe what it's like losing a sibling and having to hold your parents up under the awful strain. Then, almost exactly one year later, I lost one of the biggest mentors and role models in my life. She was the person I would call when I had major life decisions to make or sometimes just to catch up and touch base with a fellow mother and church worker.

Carol was one of those people who could have been anything she wanted to be. Yet, she shone brightly as a homeschooling mom and a minister's wife in a little country church in Indiana. She faithfully served her family, her church family, and her community by loving all of us who God sent her way. On the side she published books and articles on Christian education and parenting. She always amazed me! Yet in all of this busyness, she would always take the time to listen when I would call and never say too much too soon. Thank You, God, for women like Carol!

She was always there for me and countless others, so it shook me deeply when I read on social media that her car had been swept off the road into flood waters. Many of us waited anxiously all day praying that the news would be good and that they had found her alive. Unfortunately, when word did come, we learned the terrible news that they found her body separated from her car, and she had died. I remember well trying not to let my mind image all that she would have suffered the night that it happened.

Death is hard for us to take, especially when the person is near and dear to us. Oh, what Mary went through watching Jesus be crucified! Seeing what He went through and trying to stop the raging questions in her mind as she attempted to reconcile what she was witnessing with the promise she had received from the angel over thirty years before. How she must have rejoiced the day she heard that Jesus, her precious son, was actually raised to life again!

Thank You, Father, for the resurrection of Jesus and for the promise that we too will be raised to everlasting life!

The Long-Awaited One

The Prophecies
His Resurrection

Day 17
Isaiah 60:1-3 &
Malachi 4:2

The Messiah will rise bringing light from darkness.

Isaiah 60:1-3
Arise, shine, for your light has come, and
the glory of the LORD
rises upon you.
See, darkness covers the earth
and thick darkness is over the peoples, but
the LORD rises upon you
and his glory appears over you.
Nations will come to your light,
and kings to the brightness
of your dawn.

Malachi 4:2

But for you who revere my name, the sun
of righteousness will rise with healing in its
rays. And you will go out and frolic like
well-fed calves.

Recently, I had to have a medical procedure done that
required general anesthesia in a surgical center. I was so
nervous sitting in that waiting room chair being prepped for
surgery. I must say, the surgical center was amazing. They
provided recliners with heat and massage and offered heated
blankets as you waited for the IV to be inserted and all of the
monitors to be attached. Then there was the meeting with the
anesthesiologist and the doctor who would perform the
surgery. Everyone from the nurses to the doctors went out of
their way to help me stay calm. But no matter how
considerate everyone was, I sat there thinking, "Can't I just
skip past all of this? Why doesn't life come with a fast
forward button? I just want to be on the other side." But there
was no way around getting my problem fixed without going
through the pain and the fear of the unknown. Actually, I
guess I could have skipped the procedure, but then I would
still have the problem that was causing the other very serious
health issues. The only way to the other side was going
through with it.

For Jesus, the thought of completing the work of bearing
the weight of the sins of the world on the cross must have
seemed impossible to endure. The stress was so great we are
told that He sweat drops of blood as He prayed to the Father
in the garden on the night He was betrayed. He even asked
the Father several times if it was possible to do this work any

other way. Ultimately, He submitted His will to God's will, choosing the path through the pain and the suffering. It was the only way to fully atone for our sins. It was a dark time for Jesus and for the Father as He watched His only Son suffer on our behalf. In the passage from Isaiah today, we read that darkness would cover the earth and the people, and in fact, it did cover the earth as Jesus died on the cross.

The great news though is that out of the darkness of the work of the cross, the light did dawn again as Jesus rose from the grave! Light after darkness seems like the brightest light there is, doesn't it? You're stumbling along in the darkness in the middle of the night, and suddenly you're blinded as you flip on the light switch. That's the hope we have in Jesus. The darkness will not remain dark. His light will shine as He rises again and as the passage from Malachi reminds us, "the sun of righteousness will rise with healing in its rays." What a beautiful promise! Light will conquer darkness. God's first recorded words as He brought the world into existence were, "Let there be light." And following the darkest day, God again drew light from darkness as Jesus was risen from the dead. Let Your light shine brightly, Father!

The Long-Awaited One

The Prophecies
His Resurrection

Day 18
Hosea 13:14

God's people will also be resurrected.

Hosea 13:14

I will deliver this people from
the power of the grave;
I will redeem them from death.
Where, O death, are your plagues? Where,
O grave, is your destruction?

Woohoo! Today's passage tells us that the promise of resurrection was not just for Jesus, but for us as well. What a powerful promise! To all who are grieving or have grieved for someone they loved, we know just how strong the power of the grave is. Losing those we love hits us like a ton of bricks. Then grief continues bombarding us in waves long after the initial shock has passed as we realize what life without our cherished one is going to be like. Grief can be so powerful that it robs us of joy day after day. How do we have a good day when this was their birthday and they are no longer here? How can we celebrate the holiday when it was their favorite time of year? How can we move on with our lives when they are no longer in it? Death is powerful, and grief can overwhelm. Sometimes it is the fear of our own death and the unknown that stops us in our tracks and keeps us from really living a full life. The grave destroys, and death is hard to bear.

So, this promise of life beyond the grave and power over death because of Jesus is one of the best promises God ever gave us. Oh, the comfort that is found in knowing we will see our loved ones again and our own lives do not end with this life. It is a huge comfort to all of us living in a fallen world to know that this world is not all there is. Because of Jesus, we can anticipate life beyond this world where God will be with us just as He was in the beginning. All will be made right, and Jesus Himself will be our light. Thank you, Father!

This promise is not only for our future beyond this life, it is for here and now. How differently would we live our lives today if we truly believed this promise and said with the apostle Paul, "For to me, to live is Christ and to die is gain" (Philippians 1:21). Paul is not morbidly wishing for his own death. He is saying that if the very worst thing that can happen to us, death, is no longer our biggest fear, we can live our lives fully for Jesus without fear. God wants us while we are living this life to walk in the newness of life that He gives through the freedom of having our guilt washed away. He wants us to leave our past behind and live for Him. It can be hard to live down our past; but remember, God doesn't expect you to. Everything was taken care of at the cross. We can trust His power to forgive, redeem, and give life forever!

77

The Long-Awaited One

The Prophecies - Special Day!

Day 19
Isaiah 53

A prophecy dedicated entirely to telling the full story of
what Jesus was sent to do.

Today we come to one of the most beautiful and detailed
prophecies of the Messiah. Personally, it is one of my
favorite passages in the whole Bible because of the perfect,
poetic picture of the entire plan of what our Savior would do
for us. It is so powerfully specific that it is also one of the
biggest stumbling blocks for the Jewish people who do not
accept Jesus as the Christ.

As I prepared to write this book, I did a lot of reading,
and one of the readings was from the book A Case for Christ
by Lee Strobel. In chapter ten, he shares the story of a Jewish
man coming to faith in Jesus as the Messiah. I would
encourage you to read the chapter sometime. There is
something so powerful in the stories of men and women
coming to faith. Within his time of deep searching, Pastor
Louis Lapides finally came to a place where he decided to
read the entire Old Testament to see the prophecies of the
Messiah for himself. As he read, he was stopped cold by
Isaiah 53. In his own words, this is what he saw that day.
"With clarity and specificity, in a haunting prediction

wrapped in exquisite poetry, here was the picture of a Messiah who would suffer and die for the sins of Israel and the world – all written more than 700 years before Jesus walked the earth."

Today, the passage is actually printed after the devotional. This is so you can read the passage several as the last thing you read for the day. Feel free to read it multiple times letting the words soak deep into your soul. And as you read, feel free to highlight or make notes on the side of the page as you ponder what Jesus did and what it means to your life.

Isaiah 53

Who has believed our message
and to whom has the arm of the LORD
been revealed?
He grew up before him like a tender shoot,
and like a root out of dry ground.
He had no beauty or majesty
to attract us to him,
nothing in his appearance that we
should desire him.
He was despised and rejected by mankind,
a man of suffering, and familiar with pain.
Like one from whom people hide their faces
he was despised,
and we held him in low esteem.
Surely he took up our pain
and bore our suffering,
yet we considered him punished by God,
stricken by him, and afflicted.
But he was pierced for our transgressions,

he was crushed for our iniquities;
the punishment that brought us peace
was on him,
and by his wounds we are healed.
We all, like sheep, have gone astray,
each of us has turned to our own way;
and the LORD has laid on him
the iniquity of us all.
He was oppressed and afflicted,
yet he did not open his mouth;
he was led like a lamb to the slaughter,
and as a sheep before its shearers is silent,
so he did not open his mouth.
By oppression and judgment
he was taken away.
Yet who of his generation protested?
For he was cut off from the land of the living;
for the transgression of my people
he was punished.
He was assigned a grave with the wicked,
and with the rich in his death,
though he had done no violence,
nor was any deceit in his mouth.
Yet it was the LORD's will to crush him
and cause him to suffer,
and though the LORD makes his life an
offering for sin,
he will see his offspring and prolong his days,
and the will of the LORD will prosper
in his hand.
After he has suffered,
he will see the light of life and be satisfied;
by his knowledge my righteous servant

will justify many,
and he will bear their iniquities.
Therefore, I will give him a portion
among the great,
and he will divide the spoils with the strong,
because he poured out his life unto death,
and was numbered with the transgressors.
For he bore the sin of many
and made intercession for the transgressors.

The Long-Awaited One

The Prophecies - The Messenger

Day 20
Isaiah 40:3-5 & Malachi 3:1

A messenger would come before the Messiah.

Isaiah 40:3-5

A voice of one calling:
"In the wilderness prepare
the way for the LORD;
make straight in the desert
a highway for our God.
Every valley shall be raised up,
every mountain and hill made low;
the rough ground shall become level, the
rugged places a plain.
And the glory of the LORD
will be revealed,
and all people will see it together.
For the mouth of the LORD
has spoken."

Malachi 3:1

"I will send my messenger, who will
prepare the way before me.
Then suddenly the Lord you are seeking
will come to his temple; the messenger of
the covenant whom you desire, will come,"
says the LORD Almighty.

We are getting close to the big day! There is one more
set of passages before we head into the reading of all of the
events surrounding Jesus' birth. Hopefully, seeing the
master plan as it was laid out by God through the centuries
has truly helped you ponder the significance of Jesus coming
to this earth as our Messiah. What an amazing gift we have
been given! No wonder people have chosen to celebrate His
birth with the giving of gifts. When you have been given the
greatest gift ever, you want to share that joy.

Today's passages tell us about another messenger who
would come to "prepare the way" for the coming of the
Messiah. If it wasn't enough for God to tell us so many
specific things about Jesus and His birth, life, death and
resurrection, now He says there will be a messenger sent
ahead of Jesus to help us know that the time of the Messiah
is at hand. And when you read the accounts of Jesus'
ministry in the gospels, there are beautiful pictures of John
the Baptist doing just that. It would be a fascinating study
sometime to read just the accounts of John the Baptist. But
today, we are looking specifically at the role he was sent to
play as the harbinger of the coming Messiah.

John certainly was an interesting person. We are told that he wore clothes made of camel's hair and a leather belt around his waist. He ate locusts and wild honey (Matthew 3:4). He lived a life that fulfilled his mission of calling people to repentance and pointing the way to Jesus as the Messiah. Not an easy task! He, like Jesus, was promised a long time before his appearance, but his role was simply to open the way for the Messiah. His life was never his own. He had a job to do and he knew it. "He must become greater; I must become less." (John 3:30) Talk about a job that would take humility and selflessness! But it was also a position of great honor.

Could you image being called to be the one to share with the world that the long-awaited Messiah was about to be revealed? What an honor! How amazing when we realize that it is a calling very similar to our own as Christ-followers. If Jesus is your Savior, you have a story to share that may encourage others as they are seeking for answers. If God has led you through difficult times, you have a testimony to share that will help others find hope. If God has answered your prayers in a big way, you have a story to tell that will encourage others that we serve a God who hears our prayers. If you found the answers after a period of deep searching, you have answers to share and resources to bring to light that will help others as they search for the truth only God can give. Share your story. Reflect God's light into a very dark world. I love the way Paul describes us in Philippians 2:15b-16 as "children of God" who "shine like stars in the universe as you hold out the word of life." So, I encourage you, be a light this Christmas and every day. Remember, you don't have to create the light. You are simply called to reflect the light you have received from the source of all light. Shine on!

The Long-Awaited One

The Events

Day 21
An angel visits Zechariah.

Luke 1:5-25

In the time of Herod king of Judea there was a priest named Zechariah, who belonged to the priestly division of Abijah; his wife Elizabeth was also a descendant of Aaron. Both of them were righteous in the sight of God, observing all the Lord's commands and decrees blamelessly. But they were childless because Elizabeth was not able to conceive, and they were both very old.

Once when Zechariah's division was on duty and he was serving as priest before God, he was chosen by lot, according to the custom of the priesthood, to go into the temple of the Lord and burn incense. And when the time for the burning of incense came, all the assembled worshipers were praying outside.

Then an angel of the Lord appeared to him, standing at the right side of the altar of incense. When Zechariah saw him, he was startled and was gripped with fear. But the angel said to him: "Do not be afraid, Zechariah; your prayer has been heard. Your wife Elizabeth will bear you a son, and you are to call him John. He will be a joy and delight to you, and many will rejoice because of his birth, for he will be great in the sight of the Lord. He is never to take wine or other fermented drink, and he will be filled with the Holy Spirit even before he is born. He will bring back many of the people of Israel to the Lord their God. And he will go on before the Lord, in the spirit and power of Elijah, to turn the hearts of the parents to their children and the disobedient to the wisdom of the righteous - to make ready a people prepared for the Lord."

Zechariah asked the angel, "How can I be sure of this? I am an old man and my wife is well along in years."

The angel said to him, "I am Gabriel. I stand in the presence of God, and I have been sent to speak to you and to tell you this good news. And now you will be silent and not able to speak until the day this happens, because you did not believe my words, which will come true at their appointed time."

Meanwhile, the people were waiting for Zechariah and wondering why he stayed so long in the temple. When he came out, he could not speak to them. They realized he had seen a vision in the temple, for he kept making signs to them but remained unable to speak.

When his time of service was completed, he returned home. After this his wife Elizabeth became pregnant and for five months remained in seclusion. "The Lord has done this for me," she said. "In these days he has shown his favor and taken away my disgrace among the people."

When you read the Bible, do you ever find yourself trying to figure out how you would respond in the same situation? I do all the time. I often wonder what it would be like to be in the presence of an angel. Or what would it be like to be present when Jesus Himself healed someone? Over the next few days, we will be looking at the actual events leading up to the birth of the Messiah. In those months prior to His birth, several people were visited by angels bringing them news of the upcoming events. What would that have been like? I'm sure it was overwhelming to say the least. One clue to just how overwhelming it would have been is the fact that every time someone is in the presence of an angel, the angel must calm them down with the words, "Do not be afraid." Each person in these encounters responds in a different way and with varying results. I find myself wondering, how would I respond?

In today's passage, we see the beginnings of the fulfillment of the verses we read yesterday. Today an angel visits the father of John the Baptist to announce the coming of the messenger who would lead the way to the arrival of the Messiah. What a great honor to be chosen for such an important task, but it is an honor that comes with great responsibility. And God chose a very dramatic way to reveal His plan to Zechariah.

It was an ordinary day of service. Zechariah had been chosen by lot to enter the temple and burn the incense which was the symbol of the Israelites' prayers rising before God. We know it was viewed as a huge responsibility since "the whole multitude" had gathered outside the temple to pray for him as he completed the work. But today, things did not go according to plan. An angel appeared with big news for Zechariah and God's people. What an experience, standing in the presence of an angel hearing that your whole life would be turned upside down!

Zechariah and his wife had no children. Most people of that time believed that this was a sign that they were not right with God. That's why the writer is so careful to mention that they were blameless and righteous before God. It wasn't their fault that they were unable to have children. They had done nothing to deserve barrenness. Maybe they understood that, or maybe they often wondered themselves, "why is God not blessing us with children? What have we done wrong?" People undoubtedly gave them all sorts of advice on how to fix their problem. It would most certainly be a touchy subject even if they had made peace with the situation, since the passage informs us that they were getting older. They had probably completely given up hope that a child would ever come to them. So, we can certainly understand that when the angel spoke of his wife Elizabeth having a child, Zechariah would have some questions.

The interesting thing is the way in which Zechariah voiced his questions. He not only asked how he could know this was really going to happen, but he also started listing off the reasons why it was impossible. We can assume it must have been said with a bit of an attitude because of the angel's response. "I am Gabriel. I stand in the presence of God." The angel Gabriel was reminding Zechariah that a minute ago he was afraid and overwhelmed at the angel's presence, and now he dared to question if what Gabriel had stated could really be from God? Then Gabriel informed Zechariah, that because of his unbelief, Zechariah would be punished by being unable to speak until everything had taken place. He would have to deal with his unbelief in silence. I'm sure he wished he could take back those words, but it was too late. Imagine having to leave the temple and try to explain what had just happened to him to the anxious crowds who were waiting and praying. I'm sure in the months of silence that followed he replayed the scene over and over in his mind.

But even in his unbelief, there was hope. Just because he had met the revelation with doubt, God's plan still moved forward! Isn't it comforting to know that our doubts do not rob God of His power to do exactly what He says He will do. God rarely forces His will on specific people, but He always devises a way to get His ultimate will accomplished. We can rest in the knowledge that God is in control and that He does have a plan.

*Thank You, Father, for Your faithfulness and Your
eternal plans that open the way for all people to be made
right with You.*

The Long-Awaited One

The Events

Day 22
An angel visits Mary.

Luke 1:26-56

In the sixth month of Elizabeth's pregnancy, God sent the angel Gabriel to Nazareth, a town in Galilee, to a virgin pledged to be married to a man named Joseph, a descendant of David. The virgin's name was Mary. The angel went to her and said, "Greetings, you who are highly favored! The Lord is with you."

Mary was greatly troubled at his words and wondered what kind of greeting this might be. But the angel said to her, "Do not be afraid, Mary; you have found favor with God. You will conceive and give birth to a son, and you are to call him Jesus. He will be great and will be called the Son of the Most High. The Lord God will give him the throne of his father David, and he will reign over Jacob's descendants forever; his kingdom will never end."

"How will this be," Mary asked the angel, "since I am a virgin?"

The angel answered, "The Holy Spirit will come on you, and the power of the Most High will overshadow you. So the holy one to be born will be called the Son of God. Even Elizabeth your relative is going to have a child in her old age, and she who was said to be unable to conceive is in her sixth month. For no word from God will ever fail."

"I am the Lord's servant," Mary answered. "May your word to me be fulfilled." Then the angel left her.

At that time Mary got ready and hurried to a town in the hill country of Judea, where she entered Zechariah's home and greeted Elizabeth. When Elizabeth heard Mary's greeting, the baby leaped in her womb, and Elizabeth was filled with the Holy Spirit. In a loud voice she exclaimed: "Blessed are you among women, and blessed is the child you will bear! But why am I so favored, that the mother of my Lord should come to me? As soon as the sound of your greeting reached my ears, the baby in my womb leaped for joy. Blessed is she who has believed that the Lord would fulfill his promises to her!"

And Mary said:

"My soul glorifies the Lord and my spirit rejoices in God my Savior, for he has been mindful of the humble state of his servant. From now on all generations will call me blessed, for the Mighty One has done great things for me –
holy is his name.

His mercy extends to those who fear him, from generation to generation. He has performed mighty deeds with his arm; he has scattered those who are proud in their inmost thoughts. He has brought down rulers from their thrones but has lifted up the humble. He has filled the hungry with good things but has sent the rich away empty. He has helped his servant Israel, remembering to be merciful to Abraham and his descendants forever, just as he promised our ancestors."

Mary stayed with Elizabeth for about three months and then returned home.

This encounter with an angel is probably my favorite. The way Mary receives the news of God's plan for her life is a response that I would pray that I could give. Once again, fear and wonder are the initial reaction. But Mary waits to reply until the whole plan is laid out. Then she asks a simple question, "How can this be, since I am a virgin?" Notice her question was answered with gentleness and an uplifting word instead of punishment like Zechariah. In answer to her question, the angel describes the plan again in more detail and then uses her cousin Elizabeth's pregnancy as an encouragement. Even the barren woman is now having a child!

But Mary's calling was even more special. Her child would truly have a heavenly Father. She would be the mother of God's Son! How amazing and overwhelming! Yet she answers with a calm declaration, submitting herself to God's will. Then the angel left her, and she hurried off to see her cousin Elizabeth. On her arrival, the baby who Elizabeth was carrying leaped in her womb. Wow! Even in the womb, John was set apart and recognized the Messiah. Then Elizabeth is filled with the knowledge that Mary has been chosen for the most amazing honor. How incredible is that?

Then we read Mary's absolutely beautiful prayer. It begins with pure praise and then enumerates a litany of the greatness of God's character. She calls on His faithfulness in the past to gain perspective that God always keeps His promises. Like the angel told her, "no word from God will ever fail."

Today, an excellent activity would be to spend some time reading Mary's prayer again. As you read, notice the character qualities of God that Mary calls upon. Then take a moment to create a prayer of your own recalling the ways God has been faithful to you and revealed Himself to you in the past. It's an inspiring way to be reminded of God's constancy. May we all be encouraged that God's faithfulness never ends and never fails. He's got your whole life in His hands. You can place your trust in Him fully, every day! Now that's a gift that can excite all of us!

The Long-Awaited One

Day 23

John the Baptist is born.

Luke 1:57-80

When it was time for Elizabeth to have her baby, she gave birth to a son. Her neighbors and relatives heard that the Lord had shown her great mercy, and they shared her joy.

On the eighth day they came to circumcise the child, and they were going to name him after his father Zechariah, but his mother spoke up and said, "No! He is to be called John."

They said to her, "There is no one among your relatives who has that name."

Then they made signs to his father, to find out what he would like to name the child. He asked for a writing tablet, and to everyone's astonishment he wrote, "His name is John." Immediately his mouth was opened and his tongue set free, and he began to speak, praising God. All the

95

neighbors were filled with awe, and throughout the hill country of Judea people were talking about all these things. Everyone who heard this wondered about it, asking, "What then is this child going to be?" For the Lord's hand was with him.

His father Zechariah was filled with the Holy Spirit and prophesied:

"Praise be to the Lord, the God of Israel, because he has come to his people and redeemed them. He has raised up a horn of salvation for us in the house of his servant David (as he said through his holy prophets of long ago), salvation from our enemies and from the hand of all who hate us - to show mercy to our ancestors and to remember his holy covenant, the oath he swore to our father Abraham: to rescue us from the hand of our enemies, and to enable us to serve him without fear in holiness and righteousness before him all our days.
And you, my child, will be called a prophet of the Most High; for you will go on before the Lord to prepare the way for him, to give his people the knowledge of salvation through the forgiveness of their sins, because of the tender mercy of our

God, by which the rising sun will come to us from heaven to shine on those living in darkness and in the shadow of death, to guide our feet into the path of peace."
And the child grew and became strong in spirit; and he lived in the wilderness until he appeared publicly to Israel.

Times of waiting - we all hate them, don't we? So often, when God calls His people to do something special for Him, there is a period of waiting involved. During their time of waiting, all they had to sustain them was the direct promise from God. So difficult!

For Zechariah, it had been a year of not being able to speak. So, not only was he waiting and waiting, but he was limited in how he could express himself as he anticipated his son's birth. He had to stay silent even as he wanted to shout to the world that God had chosen him to be the father of the messenger sent ahead of the Messiah. He and Elizabeth had spent years longing for a child. And now that he was blessed with the promise of a child that was chosen of God, he couldn't tell anyone. How frustrating!

So, you can imagine his joy at having his voice set free! But first, he had to silently watch his wife go through labor as all of their friends and family gathered to share their joy. And when the time came to name the child, people tried to intervene and tell them what to name the child. Elizabeth spoke up, but everyone looked to Zechariah to determine if they were truly going to go against tradition and name the child John when no one in either family had that name.

Zechariah had doubted Gabriel before and was struck mute, so he certainly didn't want things to go wrong this time. So, he quickly wrote the name John. Immediately he regained his voice! This time he would not waste his words. He opened his mouth in praise to the One who, despite Zechariah's doubts and fears, remained true to His word. Zechariah's words were pure praise and a declaration of all that God had revealed that his son John would be. He had waited a year to share with the world that his son would be a prophet of the One true God. It must have felt amazing!

May we be just as willing to share the many ways that God has surely blessed us. Tell your friends and family when God answers your prayers. Share with the world how God has changed you from the inside out. Tell people when God brings you through what felt like an impossible situation. Share the answers you have found to the deep questions of life. Tell the world of His faithfulness!

Thank you, Father, for the promises of Your Word that sustain through our times of waiting. Thank You for taking our trials and turning them into testimonies of Your goodness and faithfulness. Thank You for using us to accomplish Your will even when we don't always trust as fully as we should. Grow our faith, Father. Great is Your faithfulness!

The Long-Awaited One

The Events

Day 24
The angel visits Joseph.

Matthew 1:18-25

This is how the birth of Jesus the Messiah came about: His mother Mary was pledged to be married to Joseph, but before they came together, she was found to be pregnant through the Holy Spirit. Because Joseph her husband was faithful to the law, and yet did not want to expose her to public disgrace, he had in mind to divorce her quietly.

But after he had considered this, an angel of the Lord appeared to him in a dream and said, "Joseph son of David, do not be afraid to take Mary home as your wife, because what is conceived in her is from the Holy Spirit. She will give birth to a son, and you are to give him the name Jesus, because he will save his people from their sins."

All this took place to fulfill what the Lord had said through the prophet: "The

99

virgin will conceive and give birth to a son, and they will call him Immanuel" (which means "God with us").

When Joseph woke up, he did what the angel of the Lord had commanded him and took Mary home as his wife. But he did not consummate their marriage until she gave birth to a son. And he gave him the name Jesus.

Joseph was also visited by an angel, but not before he was given the unbelievable news by Mary that she was pregnant with the Son of God. What was he supposed to do with that news? It was completely impossible! He knew the "facts of life." Things like this didn't just happen. How could he believe her? His image of his dream girl had been shattered, and he planned to end their relationship quietly. People would talk either way, and he didn't need this in his life. He would simply walk away and let her deal with her own mess. But God had another plan.

God sent an angel in a dream to confirm Mary's story. The angel explained the plan to him, and the amazing thing is Joseph awoke the next day and moved forward with God's directions. That took incredible faith! Scientifically, this was impossible, but Joseph believed and did as he was instructed.

It is interesting that the Bible says, "when Joseph woke up." I can't imagine he had slept very much after a dream like that. Most of us would still be worried after receiving this news. Joseph's reputation was on the line. People could count nine months, so there would be gossip and assumptions made about Mary's virtue. And if they shared the news of the angels' visits with anyone, they would certainly be met with doubt. But even in the face of all of this, Joseph slept and then rose to do what God had called him to do. Pretty impressive.

Then what was the reward for his obedience? Dealing with a pregnant wife before consummating the marriage? Oh my, not much of a honeymoon! I say this and we all chuckle a bit. But the truth is, God never promises that what He calls us to do will be easy. He does promise it will all be worth it as we see God fulfill His word. God is trustworthy and faithful, and He will fulfill His plans.

The circumstances we are placed in may never be ideal, but a godly approach to them brings about abundant life even in the midst of this broken world. When we are asked to forgive that co-worker for the tenth time, we are promoting forgiveness. When we give that person with a shady past the chance to start over, we promote new beginnings. When we sacrifice so another can have their basic needs met, we promote love and brotherhood. When we pray for those who have hurt us, we learn to look at others as God sees them. God's plans are life and peace!

Thank you, Father, for Your amazing faithfulness.

Thank You that You are trustworthy and good, and all of

Your plans will come to completion.

The Long-Awaited One

The Events

Day 25

Merry Christmas! Jesus is born!

Luke 2:1-20

In those days Caesar Augustus issued a decree that a census should be taken of the entire Roman world. (This was the first census that took place while Quirinius was governor of Syria.) And everyone went to their own town to register.

So, Joseph also went up from the town of Nazareth in Galilee to Judea, to Bethlehem the town of David, because he belonged to the house and line of David. He went there to register with Mary, who was pledged to be married to him and was expecting a child. While they were there, the time came for the baby to be born, and she gave birth to her firstborn, a son. She wrapped him in cloths and placed him in a manger, because there was no guest room available for them.

And there were shepherds living out in the fields nearby, keeping watch over their flocks at night. An angel of the Lord appeared to them, and the glory of the Lord shone around them, and they were terrified. But the angel said to them, "Do not be afraid. I bring you good news that will cause great joy for all the people. Today in the town of David a Savior has been born to you; he is the Messiah, the Lord. This will be a sign to you: You will find a baby wrapped in cloths and lying in a manger."

Suddenly a great company of the heavenly host appeared with the angel, praising God and saying,

"Glory to God in the highest heaven, and on earth peace to those on whom his favor rests."

When the angels had left them and gone into heaven, the shepherds said to one another, "Let's go to Bethlehem and see this thing that has happened, which the Lord has told us about."

So they hurried off and found Mary and Joseph, and the baby, who was lying in the manger. 17 When they had seen him, they spread the word concerning what had been told them about this child, 18 and all who heard it were amazed at what the shepherds said to them. But Mary treasured up all these things and pondered them in her heart. The shepherds returned, glorifying and praising God for all the things they had heard and seen, which were just as they had been told.

Yay! It's here! The day we've all been waiting for – Christmas day! Remember as children how hard it was to fall asleep on Christmas Eve? Then waking up really early to sneak a peek and see if Santa had actually come? I remember trying to get my dad out of bed so we could open presents - not an easy task. Great memories!

Then with my own children, I remember having to set a time limit on how early they were allowed to wake us up. Sometimes I'd hear them whispering in the hallway outside our bedroom anxiously waiting for the right time. When the time would finally come, they would run in and jump on the bed to excitedly tell us, "It's time! It's time!" Of course, there was still a little more waiting because I had to make sure my hair wasn't sticking up in every direction for the pictures. Plus, I wanted a cup of coffee and my camera by my side on the couch as we proceeded to the big event – the gifts. But first, we would gather together and read Luke chapter 2 together as a family to remind us why we celebrate and then pray together thanking God for giving us the greatest gift, Jesus. Finally, the moment arrived that the children had been anticipating – Presents!

Through the years our gift giving took on many forms, but one thing I always strived for was making sure we took the time to enjoy watching each other open and be grateful for the gifts we received. Seeing my children grow in the realization that giving the perfect gift was truly even more gratifying than getting the perfect gift. One of the ways we found to focus on giving rather than receiving was to take turns giving the next gift. My kids loved this! Now as young adults, they still find pleasure in plotting out just which gift to give next and waiting expectantly to see the recipient's reaction. What precious memories! (Just a quick disclaimer: this transition did not happen overnight!)

I pray that you and your family are making precious memories together as you unwrap the incredible gift of Jesus this year. Remember, there was a lot of waiting involved in God choosing just the right time to send His Son to walk among us. In our limited view, this plan took an inordinate amount of time and may have seemed rather slow. But God knows our hearts and deals with us patiently and wisely. Remember, Jesus was promised from the very beginning, and the moment of fulfillment was finally at hand. How exciting! As the angel told the shepherds, "I bring you good news of great joy which will be for all people. Today in the town of David a Savior has been born to you; He is Messiah, the Lord." (Luke 2:10-11)

May our hearts rejoice just like the shepherds did. May this incredible news prompt us to run to Him and worship at His feet, remembering that this day was only the beginning of all Jesus came to do. And like Mary, may we treasure up all of these things in our hearts and ponder this amazing truth - we are the recipients of the greatest gift ever given!

A **Mighty God**

who is familiar with

our weakness, yet made a way

A **Righteous Judge** who knows the

sentence we deserve, yet took our

punishment upon Himself. A **Wonderful**

Counselor who sees our daily struggle and rather

than condemn, sits at the right hand of God as our

intercessor. Our **Prince of Peace** who sees our chaos

and disorder and yet brings peace to our souls

when we abide in Him

The Way, the Truth, and the Life

Our Light, Hope, Peace, and Joy

Hallelujah!

What a Savior!

The Long-Awaited One

The Follow-Up

Day 26

Anna and Simeon see the Long-Awaited Messiah.

Luke 2:21-39

On the eighth day, when it was time to circumcise the child, he was named Jesus, the name the angel had given him before he was conceived.

When the time came for the purification rites required by the Law of Moses, Joseph and Mary took him to Jerusalem to present him to the Lord (as it is written in the Law of the Lord, "Every firstborn male is to be consecrated to the Lord"), and to offer a sacrifice in keeping with what is said in the Law of the Lord: "a pair of doves or two young pigeons."

Now there was a man in Jerusalem called Simeon, who was righteous and devout. He was waiting for the consolation of Israel, and the Holy Spirit was on him. It had been revealed to him by the Holy Spirit that he would not die before he had seen the Lord's Messiah. Moved by the Spirit, he went into the temple courts. When the parents brought in the child Jesus to do for him what the custom of the Law required, Simeon took him in his arms and praised God, saying:

"Sovereign Lord, as you have promised, you may now dismiss[c] your servant in peace.

For my eyes have seen your salvation, which you have prepared in the sight of all nations: a light for revelation to the Gentiles, and the glory of your people Israel."

The child's father and mother marveled at what was said about him. Then Simeon blessed them and said to Mary, his mother: "This child is destined to cause the falling and rising of many in Israel, and to be a sign that will be spoken against, so that the thoughts of many hearts will be revealed. And a sword will pierce your own soul too."

There was also a prophet, Anna, the daughter of Penuel, of the tribe of Asher. She was very old; she had lived with her husband seven years after her marriage, and then was a widow until she was eighty-four. She never left the temple but worshiped night and day, fasting and praying. Coming up to them at that very moment, she gave thanks to God and spoke about the child to all who were looking forward to the redemption of Jerusalem.

When Joseph and Mary had done everything required by the Law of the Lord, they returned to Galilee to their own town of Nazareth.

It had been eight days since the birth of Jesus. Mary and Joseph were doubtless absolutely exhausted. The days after the birth of a child are always crazy. The baby wakes constantly to be fed. Mary is still healing. Joseph is working to provide for his new family far from home. Neither one is getting much sleep. It was undoubtedly a very stressful time for the young parents.

Then add to the stress that the time had come for them to take the baby to Jerusalem to present the child at the temple for the purification rites of Moses, the circumcision, and the official naming of the child. Having just made the journey to Bethlehem for the census while Mary was pregnant, now they were traveling again this time with a newborn. I certainly don't envy them. But as always, God comes through with encouragement for the couple even in the midst of their stress.

In today's passage we read about two very special yet ordinary people, Simeon and Anna, who were granted the privilege of witnessing the fulfillment of the promised Messiah after years of faithful service to God. And in expressing their joy at seeing Jesus, they encouraged an exhausted Mary and Joseph that God's promise was truly being fulfilled through this baby in their arms. I'm sure that was some much-needed encouragement after the hectic events of the recent weeks and months.

Not only was this an encouragement for Mary, Joseph, Simeon, and Anna, but it also serves to encourage us. Simeon was called "righteous and devout" and He followed the Spirit of God faithfully. Anna had dedicated her whole life since becoming a widow to serving and worshipping God. They had no great positions of power or influence. They simply loved God and devoted their whole lives to following Him. They were ordinary people who were so close to God that He revealed to them in person that the Messiah had indeed come – now! How exciting for them and for us. It demonstrates to us that we don't have to have a grand, elaborate calling on our lives in order to know the heart of God. We are simply called to abide in Him and He will reveal Himself to us.

Thank you, Father, for always sending the encouragement we need to keep moving forward. Thank You that what You want most from us, is for us to abide in Your presence and draw our strength and purpose directly from You!

The Long-Awaited One

The Follow-Up

Day 27
Psalm 72:10-11; Matthew 2:1-12

The Magi arrive bearing gifts.

Psalm 72:10-11
May the kings of Tarshish and of distant shores
bring tribute to him.
May the kings of Sheba and Seba
present him gifts.
May all kings bow down to him
and all nations serve him.

Matthew 2:1-12
After Jesus was born in Bethlehem in
Judea, during the time of King Herod, Magi
from the east came to Jerusalem and asked,
"Where is the one who has been born king
of the Jews? We saw his star when it rose
and have come to worship him."

When King Herod heard this he was
disturbed, and all Jerusalem with him.
When he had called together all the

people's chief priests and teachers of the law, he asked them where the Messiah was to be born. "In Bethlehem in Judea," they replied, "for this is what the prophet has written:

'But you, Bethlehem, in the land of Judah, are by no means least among the rulers of Judah; for out of you will come a ruler who will shepherd my people Israel.

Then Herod called the Magi secretly and found out from them the exact time the star had appeared. He sent them to Bethlehem and said, "Go and search carefully for the child. As soon as you find him, report to me, so that I too may go and worship him."

After they had heard the king, they went on their way, and the star they had seen when it rose went ahead of them until it stopped over the place where the child was. When they saw the star, they were overjoyed. On coming to the house, they saw the child with his mother Mary, and they bowed down and worshiped him. Then they opened their treasures and presented him with gifts of gold, frankincense and myrrh. And having been warned in a dream not to go back to Herod, they returned to their country by another route.

One of the reasons for organizing this reading plan and writing these devotionals to supplement our reading is to give us a deeper sense of just how far-reaching God's plan for our salvation truly was and is. It was a plan so big that Magi from the east came from far away to find the new king of the Jews. They had seen his star appear in the sky and followed it in order to find Him and worship Him. That's a big deal, and Herod knew it.

It was such a big deal that Herod was worried and summoned his scholars to find out where the Messiah was to be born. And the scholars knew the answer. But unlike Simeon and Anna from yesterday's reading, they were not anxiously looking for signs of His coming. And unlike the Magi, they ignored the new, bright star and went about their business giving no heed to what was occurring unless it would threaten their own power. Herod was so distraught by what he learned that he devised a scheme to have all of the baby boys under age two killed to wipe out the threat to his throne. This was another detail that was foretold well in advance. (Matthew 2:16-18 & Jeremiah 31:15)

So, how will we respond in our every-day life to this promise of the Messiah that was fulfilled for our benefit? Will we ignore the evidence, pushing God away because we realize that to recognize Him as Messiah means He is Lord of our very lives? Or will we embrace the truth of God's great love for us demonstrated in Jesus and bow down before Him daily in reverent worship? Laying our lives at His feet as the only gift worth giving back to the One who gave everything for us.

Like the Magi, may we go to the ends of the earth to find and know our Savior. May we give the best gifts we can find to offer at His feet. They laid gold before Him to recognize that He was king on earth. They gave myrrh, an embalming oil as a symbol of death. And they gave Him frankincense, an incense, as a symbol of His deity. May we like the Magi, fully recognize what an amazing work God did for us through Jesus. May it cause us to bow before Him in wonder and awe. And may we always remember, He did it all to reconcile us to Himself. Make no mistake - our reconciliation was the reason God forged this elaborate plan right from the beginning.

Ephesians 1:3-10

Praise be to the God and Father of our Lord Jesus Christ, who has blessed us in the heavenly realms with every spiritual blessing in Christ. For he chose us in him before the creation of the world to be holy and blameless in his sight. In love he predestined us for adoption to sonship through Jesus Christ, in accordance with his pleasure and will - to the praise of his glorious grace, which he has freely given us in the One he loves. In him we have redemption through his blood, the forgiveness of sins, in accordance with the riches of God's grace that he lavished on us. With all wisdom and understanding, he made known to us the mystery of his will according to his good pleasure, which he purposed in Christ, to be put into effect when the times reach their fulfillment - to bring unity to all things in heaven and on earth under Christ.

The Long-Awaited One

The Follow-Up

Day 28
Hosea 11:1 & Matthew 2:13-15

Joseph and Mary must flee to Egypt.

Hosea 11:1

"When Israel was a child, I loved him, and out of Egypt I called my son.

Matthew 2:13-15

When they had gone, an angel of the Lord appeared to Joseph in a dream. "Get up," he said, "take the child and his mother and escape to Egypt. Stay there until I tell you, for Herod is going to search for the child to kill him."

So, he got up, took the child and his mother during the night and left for Egypt, where he stayed until the death of Herod. And so was fulfilled what the Lord had said through the prophet:

"Out of Egypt I called my son."

Do you ever feel like things have to go smoothly in order for it to be God's will? We all seem to have those thoughts at times. Things go badly in our lives, and we start to question if we have done something wrong to cause us to lose God's favor. The Bible certainly does not teach this. In fact, throughout God's Word we see examples of God revealing His plan, and yet the people involved have to go through difficult obstacles and periods of waiting before they experience God's plan coming to fruition.

David was told he would be the next king of Israel, but then he had to spend years running for his life. Joseph was given a dream, yet he had to spend years as a slave and eventually be put in prison for a crime he didn't commit before he could save his family and the people of Egypt. Abraham was promised a son in his old age, but he got so impatient waiting for the fulfillment that he tried to force the plan along by having the child with a woman other than his wife. Waiting and persevering are often a part of God's plans.

Need more proof? We have spent several weeks looking at the long-term plan God crafted to bring about the salvation of the world. But once the plan was revealed and Jesus had come, His life was threatened by Herod. Joseph was holding the long-awaited Messiah in his arms, and yet an angel came to him and told him to flee to Egypt in order to save the child's life. Then he and Mary had to wait in Egypt two years before it was safe to return. And today's passages make it clear that it was all part of the plan that was laid out through prophecy. Waiting and persevering were a part of the plan even for the Messiah. Wow!

So, the next time you are trying to accomplish something for God, whether it seems like a big thing or a little thing, let's try asking ourselves the right questions. If the task is something you know is in alignment with God's will, try not to say, "Maybe I'm not supposed to do this" or "Maybe these obstacles mean I'm not meant to do this." That's often just fear talking. Instead we should ask ourselves, "What is God trying to teach me as I move forward through this obstacle? Do I simply need to persevere and trust as I wait for God's perfect timing?" Then as you wait and pray, keep reading the Word of God. Paul's letters to the churches in the New Testament are filled with encouragement to keep our eyes on Jesus and never give up. Here is one of my favorites:

Romans 5:1-5

Therefore, since we have been justified through faith, we have peace with God through our Lord Jesus Christ, through whom we have gained access by faith into this grace in which we now stand. And we boast in the hope of the glory of God. Not only so, but we also glory in our sufferings, because we know that suffering produces perseverance; perseverance, character; and character, hope. And hope does not put us to shame, because God's love has been poured out into our hearts through the Holy Spirit, who has been given to us.

The Long-Awaited One

The Follow-Up

Day 29
Ezekiel 36:24-29a

The purpose – our salvation!

Ezekiel 36:24-29a

For I will take you out of the nations; I will gather you from all the countries and bring you back into your own land. I will sprinkle clean water on you, and you will be clean; I will cleanse you from all your impurities and from all your idols. I will give you a new heart and put a new spirit in you; I will remove from you your heart of stone and give you a heart of flesh. And I will put my Spirit in you and move you to follow my decrees and be careful to keep my laws. Then you will live in the land I gave your ancestors; you will be my people, and I will be your God. I will save you from all your uncleanness.

It's always a little sad when it's time to put away all of the Christmas decorations. Not just because of all of the packing away and cleaning up, but because it means Christmas is over. For some of us, the decorations were dismantled and stored in the attic a day or two after the festivities ended. For others, remnants of Christmas are left out for weeks or even months. My neighbor leaves their lights up all year! No matter when you decide to put everything away, it's a necessary part of the celebration. We must clear away the remnants of one celebration to make way for the new. It would be hard to celebrate spring with "Winter Wonderland" playing in the background. It would be odd to commemorate Easter around a droopy, brown, dried-up Christmas tree. We trade in our nativities for an empty tomb. We replace our rejoicing about a birth for the sadness of a cross that led to the ultimate celebration of resurrection.

In today's passage we see Ezekiel writing about God's plan for our salvation in a beautiful word picture. God promises that He will purify our hearts, cleansing us from impurities. Then when we are clean, He promises to give us a brand-new heart and spirit in place of the old. Certainly, exchanging our dead, sinful hearts for something pristine that comes directly from God is a fabulous trade-off. We are now spotless, pure, free! We have a new heart and we don't have to live our lives on our own. He promises that His Spirit will dwell in us to lead and guide us. What beautiful promises!

Have you accepted this amazing gift of God? Have you allowed Him to do His work in you and give you a new heart? If not, don't wait any longer to trade in your old life for the new life He offers. There is nothing that brings peace in this life like the redeeming power of our God and the work that was done for us on the cross. Call on His name and put your faith in the precious promises of salvation in the name of Jesus.

If you have already received this amazing gift, are you abiding in Him and allowing the Holy Spirit to guide and direct your daily life? Too often we forget to access the power of the Holy Spirit. We try to do things on our own only to be reminded of our desperate need for the guidance, direction, peace and presence that only God offers. It's only when we abide fully in God that we live the abundant life that Jesus promised to us.

In John chapter 15, Jesus describes a beautiful picture of how we should live. He is the vine, and we are the branches. Apart from Him we can do nothing. When we abide in His presence, He works in and through us to produce the most amazing fruit.

So, I urge you today. Check your heart. Once you have found the amazing gift of salvation, the gift you did nothing to earn or deserve, live in the light of the promise of a new, clean heart. And abide in His presence, seeking Him for all that you need.

Father, we thank you for new beginnings. Like the new year, a flipping of a page on the calendar, may we live with a sense of newness and freshness. A sense of peace and purpose that allows us to live abundant lives that bring You honor and glory.

The Long-Awaited One

The Follow-Up

Day 30
Daniel 7:13-14

The final part of the plan is still to come.

Daniel 7:13-14

In my vision at night I looked, and there before me was one like a son of man, coming with the clouds of heaven. He approached the Ancient of Days and was led into his presence. He was given authority, glory and sovereign power; all nations and peoples of every language worshiped him. His dominion is an everlasting dominion that will not pass away, and his kingdom is one that will never be destroyed.

As we start a new year remembering the incredible plan of God that we have been focusing on for the last month, we are reminded of just how vast, mighty, and awesome God's plans truly are. He arranged His plan for our salvation thousands of years in advance and then wove each phase together in its own perfect timing. We serve an amazingly coordinated God! I pray that taking time to read so many of the prophecies and looking at how God fulfilled them has strengthened your trust in His faithfulness.

So, why did God go to all of this trouble on our behalf? It's because of His great love for us, His creation. Josh McDowell explains it brilliantly in his book A Ready Defense:

> "He (God) wanted Jesus Christ to have all the credentials He needed when He came into the world. Yet the most exciting thing about Jesus Christ is that He came to change lives. He alone proved the hundreds of Old Testament prophecies that described His coming to be correct. He alone can fulfill the greatest prophecy of all for those who accept it – the promise of new life: "I will give you a new heart and put a new spirit within you" (Ezekiel 36:25-27). "Therefore, if any man is in Christ, he is a new creature; the old things passed away; behold, new things have come" (2 Corinthians 5:17)."

Such an amazing realization! God went to a lot of trouble to renew a relationship with us. It's exciting to know we are now cleansed, redeemed, and restored. But God's plan is not finished yet! All we have to do is look around us to see that this world is not a perfect paradise. Ultimately God will create a new heaven and a new earth, and Jesus will come again to live among us in a kingdom that will never end. Now that's a precious promise!

Prophecies about Jesus coming again start in the Old Testament and continue throughout the New Testament. It would be fun to do a study of those passages sometime. Today, however, we'll just focus on the fact that God's plan will not be complete until He has established a complete reboot of the world as we know it, making all things as they were intended to be at creation. God is so intent on us understanding that there is more to come that He gave us an entire book called Revelation dedicated to the final part of His plan.

If you've ever read the book of Revelation, you know that parts of it can seem rather hard to understand. Entire books have been written trying to interpret the book's full meaning. It can be bit overwhelming to speculate on all of the details, but we do know that in the end, God will make everything clear. The most important thing to remember is that God is victorious in the end, and those who call Him Lord will be given eternal life. Someday, we will look back on the second coming of Jesus with 20/20 vision, praising God once again for His faithfulness in completing His plan just as we have been doing as we celebrated all that He did in sending our Messiah, Jesus.

We praise You, Father, for Your incredible faithfulness that assures us that You have done all that You promised before, and You will continue to uphold and fulfill Your Word.

Reflection & Discussion Questions – Days 1-5

Prophecies of the Messiah

Days 1-5 – Look over your list of descriptions of the Messiah that you created from the first five days. Which descriptive words used by the writers were the most powerful to you? Explain your choices.

Day 1

- Do you look forward to Christmas? Why or why not?
- Does it surprise you to realize that the plan for our salvation was first revealed at the fall of man? How so?

Day 2

- Why is a strong foundation important?
- How does realizing Jesus was the foundation of God's plan help you understand the heart of God?

Day 3

- Have you ever had to call on God to be your judge so that you could let go of anger and the need for revenge?

Day 4

- What does it mean to you to realize that you have an advocate/priest in Jesus who is at God's right hand?

- Was there ever a time that you thought that you couldn't go to God? Why?

Day 5

- Which of the names of the Messiah in Isaiah 9 is the most powerful to you? Why?

Reflection & Discussion Questions – Days 6-9

Prophecies of Messiah's Birth & Life

Days 6-9 – Looking over the list of facts you recorded from the passages about Messiah's birth and life, what details surprised you? Why?

As you noticed how detailed many of the prophecies were, does this strengthen your faith? How so?

Day 6

- Are you a camping person or a resort person?
- In what situations is it easy for you to sacrifice and serve others? In what situations is it difficult?

Day 7

- Do you think it would be good or bad to know the future? What pros and cons would there be in knowing the future?

Day 8

- Why do you think it would be difficult for the people of Jesus' hometown to accept Him as the Messiah?
- Can you think of a time when God worked in your life to bring beauty from ashes, joy from mourning, or praise from despair as we read about in Isaiah 61:3?

Day 9

- How significant is it to you that a specific day in
  Jesus' life was prophesied so clearly?
- What was the significance of the triumphal entry?

Reflection & Discussion Questions – Days 10-15

Prophecies of Messiah's Death

Days 10-15 – Which prophecies of Jesus' death strike you the most? Which passage did you find the most compelling? Explain.

Day 10

- What comfort do you gain from knowing that Jesus knows your suffering – both physical and emotional?
- Have you ever had to forgive someone who has betrayed or abandoned you?
- What encouragement can we receive from Jesus not only forgiving but also commissioning His disciples even after they had abandoned Him?
- What can we learn from this level of forgiveness?

Day 11

- What events disprove the concept of intentional fulfillment?
- What makes intentional fulfillment nearly impossible?
- How does knowing this prophecy was over 1,000 years before crucifixion was invented lend to the credibility of Jesus' claim to be Messiah?

Day 12

- In what ways does Jesus fulfill the role of the Passover Lamb?
- In what ways does the Passover foreshadow what Jesus was sent to do?
- Do you think it was a coincidence that Jesus' death occurred on the weekend of the Passover celebration? Explain.

Day 13

- What's the worst physical pain you've ever suffered?
- When you consider Romans 5:6-8, is there anyone for whom you would possibly die? Could you suffer for someone you considered undeserving?
- What actions and behaviors in your life remind you just how amazing it is that Jesus died for you?

Day 14

- Have you ever considered how you may have reacted to the events of the Passover weekend?
- Whatever our reactions may have been, isn't it great to know we serve a God of second chances? Can you think of a time when you were truly grateful for a second chance from God?

Day 15

- How can our emotions get in the way of seeing God clearly?
- How can hindsight be beneficial? How can it be a hindrance?
- Do you think this reference to Jonah was one of the things the disciples remembered as the events of the crucifixion and resurrection transpired?

Reflection & Discussion Questions – Days 16-18

Prophecies of Messiah's Resurrection

Days 16-18 – What was the significance of the resurrection? What if Jesus had not risen from the dead?

Day 16

- What are some of the thoughts and feelings you think Mary may have experienced as she watched her son die?
- Who is the closest person to you that you have lost?
- How does Jesus' resurrection give us hope?

Day 17

- Have you ever had to go through a painful experience in order to get better?
- What is the darkest place you have ever been? How bright did the light seem when it pierced the darkness?
- How does Jesus' resurrection compare to light out of darkness?

Day 18

- Have you ever been overwhelmed by grief?
- How does knowledge of the resurrection effect our outlook on life and the way we live our lives in the here-and-now?

Reflection & Discussion Questions – Day 19

Special Day – the Work of Jesus Foretold!

Day 19

- As you read Isaiah 53, did you forget that this was a prophecy written over 700 years before Jesus came, lived, and died for us?
- What are your favorite words and phrases in the passage?

Reflection & Discussion Questions – Days 20-25

The Events Leading Up to the Birth of Jesus

Day 20

- What is the significance of having a messenger come just ahead of the Messiah?
- Do you think you would have enjoyed meeting John the Baptist? Explain.
- How is the calling of John the Baptist similar to our calling as Christ-followers?

Day 21

- How do you think you would respond to being in the presence of an angel? Scared? Overwhelmed? Accepting? Questioning?
- Is it comforting to know that our responses do not ruin God's ultimate plan? Elaborate.

Day 22

- Do you think you could have responded to the angel as calmly as Mary did?
- What is your favorite part of Mary's prayer?
- Mary calls on God's character and His acts of the past as she prays. How does this help her gain perspective?
- Which of God's character traits could you call on to gain strength?

Day 23

- Have you ever had to wait a long time to reach a goal or see the fulfillment of a dream? What was the hardest part of waiting? Doubts or obstacles?
- Have you ever had to go against the wishes or plans of everyone around you in order to do what God has called you to do? Explain.

Day 24

- We aren't told much about Joseph's response to the angel, but I'm sure he had a wide range of thoughts and emotions. What are some of the things he you believe he may have considered as he pondered his response to the angel's visit?
- Has God ever helped you overcome and even thrive in what seemed like an impossible situation?

Day 25

- What are your favorite Christmas Day traditions?
- What do you imagine was the hardest part of Jesus' birth for Mary and Joseph? What was the most joyful part?

Reflection & Discussion Questions – Days 26-30

The Follow-Up

Day 26

- What kinds of challenges did Mary and Joseph face when traveling to Jerusalem with a newborn?
- Does it encourage you to know that God told two very ordinary people that His promise of a Messiah was now fulfilled? Why or why not?

Day 27

- How has it strengthened your faith to read the prophecies explaining the breadth and depth of God's plan to redeem you? How so?
- How has this knowledge effected your confidence in God and His plans?
- When you see the lengths God went to, over so much time, to reconcile you to Him so that you can have a relationship with Him, does it help you understand His great love for you? How so?
- Do you ever doubt that God could truly love you? What comforts you when you have doubts?
- How does this knowledge change how you live your life every day?

Day 28

- Do you struggle to know God's will?
- What are the biggest obstacles for you in following God's will?
- How can we handle times of waiting in order to persevere?

Day 29

- Do you get sad as you put your Christmas decorations away?
- Have you accepted the gift of God? When? Tell your story.
- Are you abiding in God like Jesus described in John chapter 15?

Day 30

- Read Revelation chapter 21. What is the thing you look forward to the most about heaven?

The Long-Awaited One

Family Activities

General Activities

These activities can be used throughout the reading plan or you can use them whenever you determine that they fit your approach to a specific day better than the activity ideas on a specific day. All of the verses in this section are taken from the New International Reader's Version.

- Copy the section dividers from the devotional portion of the book. Then, have the children create a list of themes, words, or pictures that express what they have learned about the Messiah. This can also be done in a small journal or as a poster that is hung on the wall or on the refrigerator. The goal of this activity is for the children to see just how detailed the plan for the Messiah was all in one place.

- If reading aloud together, have the students use a tablet or scrap paper to actively listen as the passages are read. Active listening is simply giving the students a place for them to jot down words, phrases, or pictures that represent the important parts of the verse as they hear it. Allow them to share what they created on their page and tell you why they chose the words or events they chose.

- If you are looking up the verses on your own, choose a single-color highlighter to mark the verses as you go.

This way you will easily see the verses and remember the context.

- Decorate your Christmas tree or a small separate tree with the promises about Jesus and/or shapes that represent the events that are predicted.

Examples:

- Decorate and hang themed shapes

    (angels, star, lamb, manger, sheep)

- Buy a set of plain ornaments at a craft store and decorate them with key promises about the Messiah. (We did this with the names of Messiah given in Isaiah chapter 9)

- OR mix and match using a variety of themes

Days 1-5 - The Messiah

<u>Days 1-5</u> – Throughout these 5 days, create a poster to hang or use a white board or chalkboard to keep a running list of the key words used to describe the coming Messiah.

Day 1

Genesis 3:15

I will make you and the woman hate each other. Your children and her children will be enemies. Her son will crush your head. And you will bite his heel."

Key Point: Even though Adam and Eve disobeyed God and there would be consequences to pay, He let them know that He had a plan to take care of the problem of sin in the future.

Genesis 12:1-3

The LORD had said to Abram, "Go from your country, your people and your father's family. Go to the land I will show you. "I will make you into a great nation. And I will bless you. I will make your name great.

You will be a blessing to others. I will
bless those who bless you. I will put a curse
on anyone who puts a curse on you. All
nations on earth will be blessed because of
you."

Key Point: One of the earliest parts of God revealing His plan for a Messiah was choosing Abram to be the leader of a group of people who God would call His own. God set Abram apart by changing his name to Abraham and promising him a son, even though he was already an old man who had no children. Then through Abraham's family line, God would send the Messiah to complete the work that would make a way for the entire world to return to Him.

- Look up the definition of the word Messiah. Discuss what this means to you. To help facilitate discussion, create a chart with boxes for all or some of the following: the definition found online, a drawing, characteristics, examples, and your own wording for the definition. If doing this in a small group setting, split into groups to make the charts. Then create a definition as a group.
- Discussion: What are the most exciting parts of Christmas?
- Discussion: The promise of a Messiah was given *after* Adam and Eve had disobeyed. Do you think it's important to know that you can be forgiven when you've done the wrong thing?

- Child-led discussion – Place a series of questions for the children to ask their parents or grandparents in a bowl or bag. Have them draw a question and ask it. Here are some fun ones to get you started:
  - What was Christmas like when you were a child?
  - What traditions did you have to help you celebrate? Which traditions did you love? Were there any you didn't like?
  - What was the best gift you ever received?
  - Which do you like more, getting presents or giving presents?
  - When did the meaning of Christmas become important to you?

Day 2

Psalm 118:21-23

LORD, I will give thanks to you, because
you answered me.
You have saved me.
The stone the builders didn't accept
has become the most important
stone of all.
The LORD has done it. It is wonderful in
our eyes.

Isaiah 28:16

So the LORD and King speaks.
He says, "Look! I am laying a stone in
Zion. It is a stone that has been tested.
It is the most important stone for a firm
foundation. The one who depends on that
stone will never be shaken.

Key Point: Sending the Messiah would be the foundation of everything God planned to do in order to have a relationship with us.

- Using building blocks of any kind, discuss the importance of a strong foundation. What does a firm foundation allow you to do?
- Build gingerbread houses. This can be done with a kit or even with plain graham crackers and frosting. Why is it important to allow the base to dry completely before putting on the roof? What would happen if you didn't build your house on an even base?

Day 3

Isaiah 11:1-5,10

Jesse's family is like a tree that has been
cut down. A new little tree will grow from
its stump.
From its roots a Branch will grow
and produce fruit.
The Spirit of the LORD will
rest on that Branch.
The Spirit will help him to be wise
and understanding.
The Spirit will help him make wise plans
and carry them out.
The Spirit will help him know the LORD
and have respect for him.
The Branch will take delight in respecting
the LORD.
He will not judge things only by the
way they look.
He won't make decisions based simply on
what people say.
He will always do what is right when he
judges those who are in need.
He'll be completely fair when he makes
decisions about poor people.
When he commands that people
be punished, it will happen.

When he orders that evil people be put to
death, it will take place.
He will put on godliness as if it
were his belt.
He'll wear faithfulness around his waist.
At that time, here is what the man who is
called the Root of Jesse will do.
He will be like a banner
that brings nations together.
They will come to Him.
And the place where He rules
will be glorious.

Isaiah 16:5

A man from the royal house of David will
sit on Judah's throne.
He will rule with faithful love.
When he judges he will do what is fair.
He will be quick to do what is right.

Key Point: God continues to pass the promise of a
Messiah on through Abraham's family line. The Messiah
would be a righteous, fair judge.

- Discussion: What would happen in a sport without
  referees? What if the referees were unfair?
- Bake something without the directions. How did it turn
  out?

- Create a game together. What rules were needed to keep the game running smoothly?
- Play one of your favorite board games but omit one or two of the key rules. How did it turn out?

Day 4

Psalm 110:1-4

The LORD says to my lord,
"Sit at my right hand until I put your
enemies under your control."
The LORD will make your royal authority
spread out from Zion to other lands.
He says, "Rule over your enemies
who are all around you."
Your troops will be willing to fight for you
on the day of battle.
Your young men will be
wrapped in holy majesty.
They will come to you like the fresh dew
that falls early in the morning.
The LORD has made a promise.
He will not change his mind.
He has said, "You are a priest forever, just
like Melchizedek."

Key Point: The Messiah will sit at God's right hand and be our priest and king.

- Can you think of a time when you were glad to have your mom and dad intervene and handle a situation for you?

Day 5

Isaiah 9:2,6-7

The people who are now living in
darkness will see a great light.
They are now living in a very dark land.
But a light will shine on them.
A child will be born to us.
A son will be given to us.
He will rule over us.
And he will be called
Wonderful Adviser and Mighty God.
He will also be called
Father Who Lives Forever and Prince
Who Brings Peace.
There will be no limit to how
great his authority is.
The peace he brings will never end.
He will rule on David's throne
and over his kingdom.

He will make the kingdom
strong and secure.
His rule will be based on what is
fair and right.
It will last forever.
The LORD's great love will
make sure that happens.
He rules over all.

Key Point: The Messiah has many names that describe who He would be.

- Discussion: What does your name mean? Does it fit you? How?
- Discussion: What do the names of Messiah tell you about him?
- Memorize the part of verse 6 that includes the names of Messiah. (The part that is in italics) To practice, put the verse on notecards, shuffle them up and race to put the cards in order.
- Create a set of ornaments with the names of Messiah on them. (I personally prefer the names as stated in the NIV Bible translation)
- Listen to Handel's "Messiah" online. Which parts of the passage do you hear in the lyrics?

Days 6 & 7 - Messiah's Birth

Isaiah 7:14

The Lord himself will give you a sign. The
virgin is going to have a baby.
She will give birth to a son.
And he will be called Immanuel.

Key Point: Messiah will be born to a virgin. He will be
named Immanuel, which means "God with us."

- Discussion: Do you ever wish you could see God? What
  do you think it would be like to live with God every day?

Day 7

Micah 5:2-5

The LORD says, "Bethlehem Ephrathah,
you might not be an important town in the
nation of Judah.
But out of you will come for me a ruler
over Israel. His family line goes back to the
early years of your nation.
It goes all the way back to days
of long ago."

The LORD will hand over his people to
their enemies. That will last until the
pregnant woman bears her promised son.
Then the rest of his relatives in Judah will
return to their land.
That promised son will stand firm and be a
shepherd for his flock.
The LORD will give him the
strength to do it.
The LORD his God will give him the
authority to rule.
His people will live safely.
His greatness will reach from one end of
the earth to the other.
And he will be our peace.

Key Point: Messiah would be born in Bethlehem.

- Find Bethlehem, Israel on a map. Find out how big Bethlehem is compared to neighboring towns.
- Find Bethlehem on Google maps and find out how far Mary and Joseph had to walk to go from Nazareth to Bethlehem.
- Discussion: We've discussed lots of the qualities of the Messiah and today's verses listed even more. What description of Messiah do you like the most? Why?

Days 8 & 9 - Messiah's Life

Day 8

Isaiah 61:1-3

The Spirit of the LORD
and King is on me.
The LORD has anointed me to announce
good news to poor people.
He has sent me to comfort those whose
hearts have been broken.
He has sent me to announce freedom for
those who have been captured.
He wants me to set prisoners free from
their dark cells.
He has sent me to announce the year
when he will set his people free.
He wants me to announce the day when
he will pay his enemies back.
Our God has sent me to comfort all those
who are sad.
He wants me to help those in Zion who
are filled with sorrow.
I will put beautiful crowns on their heads
in place of ashes.
I will anoint them with olive oil to give
them joy instead of sorrow.
I will give them a spirit of praise in place
of a spirit of sadness.

They will be like oak trees that are strong
and straight.
The LORD himself will plant them
in the land.
That will show how glorious he is.

Key Point: Messiah would live to help people.

- Make a crown. Verse three says Messiah would give us beautiful crowns. How does it feel to get something really great that you know you don't deserve?
- Discussion: What part of Jesus' works on earth would you have enjoyed getting to see first-hand? (Miracles? Teaching? Healing? Praying? Having dinner together?)

Day 9

Zechariah 9:9

"City of Zion, be full of joy!
People of Jerusalem, shout!
See, your king comes to you.
He always does what is right.
He has won the victory.
He is humble and riding on a donkey. He
is sitting on a donkey's colt.

Psalm 118:26-28

Blessed is the one who comes in the name
of the LORD.
From the temple of the LORD
we bless you.
The LORD is God.
He has been good to us.
Take branches in your hands.
Join in the march on the day
of the feast.
March up to the corners of the altar.
You are my God, and I will praise you.
You are my God, and I will honor you.

Key Point: God told us about Palm Sunday, the day Jesus would enter Jerusalem and the people would celebrate Him as the coming Messiah.

- Look up the event of Palm Sunday in one of the New Testament accounts and compare it to today's passages. (Matthew 21:1-9; Mark 11:1-10; Luke 19:28-39; John 12:12-18)
- Discussion: Would you have liked to have been in the crowd on Palm Sunday? Why or why not?
- Make palm branches and act out the scene.

Days 10-14 - Messiah Would Die for Us

Day 10

Psalm 41:9

Even my close friend, someone I trusted,
has failed me.
I even shared my bread with him.

Zechariah 11:12-13

I told them, "If you think it is best, give
me my pay. But if you don't think so, keep
it." So, they paid me 30 silver coins. The
LORD said to me, "Throw those coins to
the potter." That amount shows how little
they valued me! So, I threw the 30 silver
coins to the potter at the LORD's temple.

Zechariah 13:7

"My sword, wake up!
Attack my shepherd!
Attack the man who is close to me,"
announces the LORD who rules over all.
"Strike down the shepherd.
Then the sheep will be scattered.
And I will turn my hand against their little
ones.

Key Point: Messiah would be betrayed and abandoned.

- Have you ever been hurt or betrayed by a friend? Jesus was betrayed by His closest friends and followers. How do you think Jesus felt as His friends walked away when He needed them most?
- Make a list of what a good friend does when a friend is having a hard time.

Day 11

Psalm 22:1,7-8,16-18

My God, my God,
why have you deserted me?
Why do you seem so far away when I need
you to save me?
Why do you seem so far away that you
can't hear my groans?
All those who see me laugh at me.
They shout at me and make fun of me.
They shake their heads at me.
They say, "He trusts in the LORD. Let the
LORD help him.
If the LORD is pleased with him,
let him save him."

A group of sinful people has
closed in on me.
They are all around me like a
pack of dogs.
They have pierced my hands
and my feet.
Everyone can see all my bones right
through my skin.
People stare at me.
They laugh when I suffer.
They divide up my clothes among them.
They cast lots for what I am wearing.

Key Points: God revealed many details of how the Messiah would die for us so we would recognize Him when He came.

- Set up dominoes in patterns. Discuss how each domino had to be in exactly the right spot for each of them to fall correctly to complete the pattern. How is this similar to what God did in arranging the coming of the Messiah?

Day 12

Exodus 12:3,5-7,12-14, 46

Speak to the whole community of Israel.
Tell them that on the tenth day of this
month each man must get a lamb from his
flock. A lamb should be chosen for each
family and home. The animals you choose
must be males that are a year old. They
must not have any flaws. You may choose
either sheep or goats.

Take care of them until the 14th day of
the month. Then the whole community of
Israel must kill them when the sun goes
down. Take some of the blood. Put it on the
sides and tops of the doorframes of the
houses where you eat the lambs.

"That same night I will pass through
Egypt. I will strike down all those born first
among the people and animals. And I will
judge all the gods of Egypt. I am the LORD.
The blood on your houses will be a sign for
you. When I see the blood, I will pass over
you. No deadly plague will touch you when
I strike Egypt.

Always remember this day. You and your
children after you must celebrate this day
as a feast to honor the LORD. You must do

this for all time to come. It is a law that will
last forever.
"It must be eaten inside the house. Do not
take any of the meat outside. Do not break
any of the bones."

Key Point: In order to set His people free from slavery in
Egypt, God laid out a plan called the Passover. He prescribed
a dinner for them to share just before God would set them
free in a dramatic way. Part of the process was for the family
to paint their door in the blood of the lamb. This would set
them apart when the big event happened, saving their whole
household from God's wrath. God's people were to continue
celebrating the event every year in remembrance of what He
had done for them. The Messiah would be just like the
Passover Lamb so God could set all people free.

- Discuss the story of the Passover (Exodus 11-12)
- Make a Lamb craft.
- Celebrate a mock Passover feast.
- Discussion: How was Jesus just like the Passover Lamb?

Day 13

Isaiah 52:13-15

The LORD says,
"My servant will act wisely and
accomplish his task.
He will be highly honored.
He will be greatly respected.
Many people were shocked
when they saw him.
He was so scarred that he no longer
looked like a person.
His body was so twisted that he did not
look like a human being anymore.
But many nations will be surprised when
they see what he has done.
Kings will be so amazed that they will not
be able to say anything.
They will understand things
they were never told.
They will know the meaning of things
they never heard."

Key Point: The Messiah would suffer terribly for us.

- Discussion: Have you ever been badly hurt? Have you ever seen someone who was badly hurt? How did they look and feel? Jesus was hurt so badly that it was hard to recognize Him. Knowing that He suffered so much, can you imagine how much He must love you?

Day 14

Zechariah 12:10-13:1

"I will pour out a spirit of grace and prayer on David's family line. I will also send it on those who live in Jerusalem. They will look to me. I am the one they have pierced. They will mourn over me as someone mourns over an only child who has died. They will be full of sorrow over me. Their sorrow will be just like someone's sorrow over an oldest son. At that time there will be a lot of weeping in Jerusalem. It will be as great as the weeping of the people at Hadad Rimmon. Hadad Rimmon is in the valley of Megiddo. They were weeping over Josiah's death. Everyone in the land will mourn. Each family will mourn by themselves and their wives by themselves. That will include the family lines of David, Nathan, Levi, Shimei and all the others. "At that time a fountain will be opened for the benefit of David's family line. It will also bless the others who live in Jerusalem.

It will wash away their sins. It will make
them pure and 'clean.'

Key Point: God's people would be sad once they saw the
Messiah die, but His death would cleanse them from their
sins.

- Make a cross craft.
- Read Matthew 27:32-56, or Mark 15:1-39. Draw the
  scene of the three crosses on a hill. How would it feel to
  see Jesus suffer for you?

Days 15-19 – Messiah Would Rise Again

Day 15

Matthew 12:38-40

Some of the Pharisees and the teachers
of the law came to Jesus.
They said, "Teacher, we want to see a
sign from you."
He answered, "Evil and unfaithful
people ask for a sign! But none will be
given except the sign of the prophet Jonah.
Jonah was in the belly of a huge fish for
three days and three nights. Something like
that will happen to the Son of Man. He will
spend three days and three nights in the
grave.

Key Point: Jesus predicted that He would have to die, be
buried, and be raised to life again by using the example of
Jonah who spent three days and three nights in the belly of a
great fish when he ran from God's calling.

• Read Jonah 1-2. Draw a life cycle diagram of the events.

- Make a big fish and place a Jonah character inside. Tell the basic story. You could read the story in the first two chapters of the book of Jonah in the Old Testament
  - •Discussion: How was Jesus like Jonah who spent three days and nights in the belly of the fish?

Day 16

Psalm 16:8-11

I keep my eyes always on the LORD.
He is at my right hand.
So I will always be secure.
So my heart is glad.
Joy is on my tongue.
My body also will be secure.
You will not leave me
in the place of the dead.
You will not let your faithful one
rot away.
You always show me the path of life.
You will fill me with joy
when I am with you.
You will make me happy forever
at your right hand.

Key Point: Messiah would not stay dead!

- Discussion: How cool do you think it would be to see someone come back from the dead?
- Make a tomb or a resurrection garden.

Day 17

Isaiah 60:1-3

"People of Jerusalem, get up.
Shine, because your light has come. The
glory of the LORD will shine on you.
Darkness covers the earth.
Thick darkness spreads
over the nations.
But I will rise and shine on you.
My glory will appear over you.
Nations will come to your light.
Kings will come to the brightness of your
new day.

Malachi 4:2

But here is what will happen for you who
have respect for me.
The sun that brings life will rise.
Its rays will bring healing to my people.
You will go out and leap for joy like calves
that have just been fed.

Key Point: Messiah would come back from the dead.

- Make a bright light display in a dark room using tree lights, lamps, flashlights, or cell phones.
- Discussion: How great is light out of darkness? Go in a dark room or closet and come out quickly. How does the darkness make you feel? The light? God tells us Jesus will be our light. How cool!

Day 18

Hosea 13:14

"I will set these people free from the
power of the grave.
I will save them from death.
Death, where are your plagues?
Grave, where is your power to destroy?

Key Point: Because Jesus rose again, we will also rise from the dead.

- Discussion: Dying is so sad. Have you ever had a pet or someone you know die? We miss them so much! But God promises that because of Jesus, we can be raised to new life. How exciting! How does that make you feel?

164

- Activity: Do you know anyone who is sad this Christmas season because they are missing loved ones? Send them a Christmas card, an encouraging note, or bake them a special treat to let them know they are not alone.

Day 19 - Special Day

Isaiah 53

Who has believed what we've been
saying? Who has seen the LORD's saving
power?
His servant grew up like a
tender young plant.
He grew like a root coming up out of dry
ground.
He didn't have any beauty or majesty that
made us notice him.
There wasn't anything special about the
way he looked that drew us to him. People
looked down on him.
They didn't accept him.
He knew all about pain and suffering. He
was like someone people turn their faces
away from.
We looked down on him.
We didn't have any respect for him.
He suffered the things
we should have suffered.

He took on himself the pain that should
have been ours.
But we thought God was punishing him.
We thought God was wounding him and
making him suffer.
But the servant was pierced
because we had sinned.
He was crushed
because we had done what was evil.
He was punished
to make us whole again.
His wounds have healed us.
All of us are like sheep.
We have wandered away from God.
All of us have turned to our own way. And
the LORD has placed on his servant the sins
of all of us.
He was treated badly
and made to suffer.
But he didn't open his mouth.
He was led away
like a lamb to be killed.
Sheep are silent while their wool is being
cut off.
In the same way,
he didn't open his mouth.
He was arrested
and sentenced to death.
Then he was taken away.

He was cut off from this life.
He was punished
for the sins of my people.
Who among those who were living
at that time tried to stop
what was happening?
He was given a grave with those
who were evil.
But his body was buried in the tomb of a
rich man.
He was killed even though he hadn't
harmed anyone.
And he had never lied to anyone.
The LORD says, "It was my plan to crush
him and cause him to suffer.
I made his life an offering to pay for sin.
But he will see all his children after him. In
fact, he will continue to live.
My plan will be brought about
through him.
After he has suffered,
he will see the light of life.
And he will be satisfied.
My godly servant
will make many people godly
because of what he will accomplish.
He will be punished for their sins.
So I will give him a place of honor among
those who are great.

He will be rewarded
just like others who win the battle. That's
because he was willing to give his life as a
sacrifice.
He was counted among those who had
committed crimes.
He took the sins of many people
on himself.
And he gave his life for those who had
done what is wrong."

Key Point: God sent the Messiah to redeem us.

- Read today's verses several times. Highlight the words that stand out to you. What phrases make you sad? Why? What phrases give you hope? Why?
- This would be a particularly great day to do an active listening page as you read aloud.

Days 20 & 21 - A Messenger

Day 20

Malachi 3:1

The LORD who rules over all says, "
I will send my messenger.
He will prepare my way for me.
Then suddenly the Lord you are looking
for will come to his temple.
The messenger of the covenant will come.
He is the one you long for."

Isaiah 40:3-5

A messenger is calling out,
"In the desert prepare the way for the
LORD. Make a straight road through it for
our God.
Every valley will be filled in.
Every mountain and hill
will be made level.
The rough ground will be smoothed out.
The rocky places will be made flat.
Then the glory of the LORD will appear.
And everyone will see it together.
The LORD has spoken."

Key Point: God would send another messenger who would come before the Messiah to help us recognize the Messiah.

- Play a messenger game. In Ancient Rome, one of the ways secret messages were passed behind enemy lines used a strip of paper and two dowel rods. The messenger and the receiver each had a stick of the equal diameter. The messenger would wrap the paper around their stick at an angle moving down the stick. Then, he would write the message vertically down the stick. This made the strip of paper virtually unreadable when unwrapped and carried as a folded piece of paper. But the message could be read clearly when taken to the waiting receiver and wrapped around the second stick of equal diameter. Try this out with the message, "Good news! Messiah is coming!" How well did it work? Take some time to decide how you would deliver such an important message if you were John the Baptist.

- Take some time to decide how you would deliver such an important message if you were John the Baptist.

Day 21

Luke 1:5-25

Herod was king of Judea. During the time he was ruling, there was a priest named Zechariah. He belonged to a group of priests named after Abijah. His wife Elizabeth also came from the family line of Aaron. Both of them did what was right in the sight of God. They obeyed all the Lord's commands and rules faithfully. But they had no children, because Elizabeth was not able to have any. And they were both very old.

One day Zechariah's group was on duty. He was serving as a priest in God's temple. He happened to be chosen, in the usual way, to go into the temple of the Lord. There he was supposed to burn incense. The time came for this to be done. All who had gathered to worship were praying outside.

Then an angel of the Lord appeared to Zechariah. The angel was standing at the right side of the incense altar. When Zechariah saw him, he was amazed and terrified. But the angel said to him, "Do not be afraid, Zechariah. Your prayer has been heard. Your wife Elizabeth will have a child. It will be a boy, and you must call him John. He will be a joy and delight to you. His birth will make many people very glad. He will be important in the sight of the Lord. He must never drink wine or other such drinks. He will be filled with the Holy Spirit even before he is born. He will bring back many of the people of Israel to the Lord their God. And he will prepare the way for the Lord. He will have the same spirit and power that Elijah had. He will bring peace between parents and their children. He will teach people who don't obey to be wise and do what is right. In this way, he will prepare a people who are ready for the Lord."

Zechariah asked the angel, "How can I be sure of this? I am an old man, and my wife is old too."

The angel said to him, "I am Gabriel. I serve God. I have been sent to speak to you and to tell you this good news. And now you will have to be silent. You will not be able to speak until after John is born. That's because you did not believe my words. They will come true at the time God has chosen."

During that time, the people were waiting for Zechariah to come out of the temple.

They wondered why he stayed there so long. When he came out, he could not speak to them. They realized he had seen a vision in the temple. They knew this because he kept gesturing to them. He still could not speak.

When his time of service was over, he returned home. After that, his wife Elizabeth became pregnant. She stayed at home for five months. "The Lord has done this for me," she said. "In these days, he has been kind to me. He has taken away my shame among the people."

Key Point: An angel tells Zechariah that he and Elizabeth would be the parents of the messenger who would prepare the way for the Messiah.

- Act out the scene.
- Play charades. How hard is it to express yourself without word? How would you act out "good news"?

Days 22-25 - The Events

General Activities – Jesus is Born!

- Make a star craft.
- Create a poster of the poem from the Day 25 devotional.
- Create a manger scene.
- The events week is a great time for the children to do active listening pages as the stories are read aloud.
- As we head into the events, take some time to discuss how amazing it is that there were so many people who carried God's Word to His people over so much time, and yet the story is one cohesive unit. Begin your discussion by trying to write a story together as a family. Start a sentence, and then have each person add a few words trying to create a story. How easy was this? Compare this to what God did in His Word.

Day 22

Luke 1:26-56

In the sixth month after Elizabeth had become pregnant, God sent the angel Gabriel to Nazareth, a town in Galilee. He was sent to a virgin. The girl was engaged to a man named Joseph. He came from the family line of David. The virgin's name was Mary. The angel greeted her and said, "The Lord has blessed you in a special way. He is with you."

Mary was very upset because of his words. She wondered what kind of greeting this could be. But the angel said to her, "Do not be afraid, Mary. God is very pleased with you. You will become pregnant and give birth to a son. You must call him Jesus. He will be great and will be called the Son of the Most High God. The Lord God will make him a king like his father David of long ago. The Son of the Most High God will rule forever over his people. They are from the family line of Jacob. That kingdom will never end."

"How can this happen?" Mary asked the angel. "I am a virgin."

The angel answered, "The Holy Spirit will come to you. The power of the Most High

God will cover you. So the holy one that is born will be called the Son of God. Your relative Elizabeth will have a child even though she is old. People thought she could not have children. But she has been pregnant for six months now. That's because what God says will always come true."

"I serve the Lord," Mary answered. "May it happen to me just as you said it would." Then the angel left her.

At that time Mary got ready and hurried to a town in Judea's hill country. There she entered Zechariah's home and greeted Elizabeth. When Elizabeth heard Mary's greeting, the baby inside her jumped. And Elizabeth was filled with the Holy Spirit. In a loud voice she called out, "God has blessed you more than other women. And blessed is the child you will have! But why is God so kind to me? Why has the mother of my Lord come to me? As soon as I heard the sound of your voice, the baby inside me jumped for joy. You are a woman God has blessed. You have believed that the Lord would keep his promises to you!"

Mary said, "My soul gives glory to the Lord.

My spirit delights in God my Savior.

He has taken note of me
even though I am not considered
important. From now on all people will call
me blessed. The Mighty One has done great
things for me. His name is holy.
He shows his mercy to those who have
respect for him, from parent to child down
through the years. He has done mighty
things with his powerful arm. He has
scattered those who are proud in their
deepest thoughts. He has brought down
rulers from their thrones. But he has lifted
up people who are not considered
important. He has filled with good things
those who are hungry. But he has sent
away empty those who are rich. He has
helped the people of Israel, who serve him.
He has always remembered to be kind to
Abraham and his children down through
the years. He has done it just as he
promised to our people of long ago." Mary
stayed with Elizabeth about three months.
Then she returned home.

Key Point: An angel visits Mary to announce that she
would be the mother of the Messiah.

• Draw what you think an angel might actually look like.

- Act out the scene.
- Compose a prayer like Mary's prayer.

Day 23

Luke 1:57-80

The time came for Elizabeth to have her baby. She gave birth to a son. 58 Her neighbors and relatives heard that the Lord had been very kind to her. They shared her joy.

On the eighth day, they came to have the child circumcised. They were going to name him Zechariah, like his father. 60 But his mother spoke up. "No!" she said. "He must be called John."

They said to her, "No one among your relatives has that name."

Then they motioned to his father. They wanted to find out what he would like to name the child. He asked for something to write on. Then he wrote, "His name is John." Everyone was amazed. Right away Zechariah could speak again. Right away he praised God. All his neighbors were filled with fear and wonder. Throughout Judea's hill country, people were talking about all these things. Everyone who heard this wondered about it.

And because the Lord was with John, they asked, "What is this child going to be?"

John's father Zechariah was filled with the Holy Spirit. He prophesied,

"Give praise to the Lord, the God of Israel!

He has come to his people and purchased their freedom. He has acted with great power and has saved us. He did it for those who are from the family line of his servant David.

Long ago holy prophets said he would do it.

He has saved us from our enemies. We are rescued from all who hate us. He has been kind to our people of long ago. He has remembered his holy covenant. He made a promise to our father Abraham. He promised to save us from our enemies.

Then we could serve him without fear.

He wants us to be holy and godly as long as we live.

"And you, my child, will be called a prophet of the Most High God. You will go ahead of the Lord to prepare the way for him. You will tell his people how they can be saved. You will tell them that their sins can be forgiven. All of that will happen because our God is tender and caring.

His kindness will bring the rising sun to us
from heaven. It will shine on those living
in darkness and in the shadow of death.
  It will guide our feet on the path of peace."
  The child grew up, and his spirit became
strong. He lived in the desert until he
appeared openly to Israel.

Key Point: The messenger, John, is born.

- Write a prayer of praise like Zechariah's.
- Discussion: What would it feel like to finally be able to talk again after such a long time of silence?

Day 24

Matthew 1:18-25

This is how the birth of Jesus the Messiah
came about. His mother Mary and Joseph
had promised to get married. But before
they started to live together, it became
clear that she was going to have a baby. She
became pregnant by the power of the Holy
Spirit. Her husband Joseph was faithful to
the law. But he did not want to put her to
shame in public. So, he planned to divorce
her quietly.

But as Joseph was thinking about this, an angel of the Lord appeared to him in a dream. The angel said, "Joseph, son of David, don't be afraid to take Mary home as your wife. The baby inside her is from the Holy Spirit. She is going to have a son. You must give him the name Jesus. That's because he will save his people from their sins."

All this took place to bring about what the Lord had said would happen. He had said through the prophet, "The virgin is going to have a baby. She will give birth to a son. And he will be called Immanuel." The name Immanuel means "God with us."

Key Point: An angel appears to tell Joseph that he should still marry Mary and that he is to name the baby Jesus.

- Make an angel and make it glow or sparkle using glow-in-the dark markers, paper, or glitter.
- Act out the scene.

Day 25

Luke 2:1-20

In those days, Caesar Augustus made a law. It required that a list be made of everyone in the whole Roman world. It was the first time a list was made of the people while Quirinius was governor of Syria. Everyone went to their own town to be listed.

So Joseph went also. He went from the town of Nazareth in Galilee to Judea. That is where Bethlehem, the town of David, was. Joseph went there because he belonged to the family line of David. He went there with Mary to be listed. Mary was engaged to him. She was expecting a baby. While Joseph and Mary were there, the time came for the child to be born. She gave birth to her first baby. It was a boy. She wrapped him in large strips of cloth. Then she placed him in a manger. That's because there was no guest room where they could stay.

There were shepherds living out in the fields nearby. It was night, and they were taking care of their sheep. An angel of the Lord appeared to them. And the glory of the Lord shone around them. They were terrified. But the angel said to them, "Do not be afraid. I bring you good news. It will bring great joy for all the people. Today in the town of David a Savior has been born to you. He is the Messiah, the Lord. Here is how you will know I am telling you the truth. You will find a baby wrapped in strips of cloth and lying in a manger."

Suddenly a large group of angels from heaven also appeared. They were praising God. They said, "May glory be given to God in the highest heaven! And may peace be given to those he is pleased with on earth!"

The angels left and went into heaven. Then the shepherds said to one another, "Let's go to Bethlehem. Let's see this thing that has happened, which the Lord has told us about."

So they hurried off and found Mary and Joseph and the baby. The baby was lying in the manger. After the shepherds had seen him, they told everyone. They reported what the angel had said about this child. All who heard it were amazed at what the shepherds said to them. But Mary kept all these things like a secret treasure in her heart. She thought about them over and over. The shepherds returned. They gave glory and praise to God. Everything they

had seen and heard was just as they had
been told.

Key Point: Jesus was born!

- Enjoy your day!!

Days 26-30 - The Follow-Up

Day 26

Luke 2:21-39

When the child was eight days old, he was circumcised. At the same time, he was named Jesus. This was the name the angel had given him before his mother became pregnant.

The time came for making Mary "clean" as required by the Law of Moses. So, Joseph and Mary took Jesus to Jerusalem. There they presented him to the Lord. In the Law of the Lord it says, "The first boy born in every family must be set apart for the Lord. They also offered a sacrifice. They did it in keeping with the Law, which says, "a pair of doves or two young pigeons."

In Jerusalem there was a man named Simeon. He was a good and godly man. He was waiting for God's promise to Israel to come true. The Holy Spirit was with him. The Spirit had told Simeon that he would not die before he had seen the Lord's Messiah. The Spirit led him into the temple courtyard. Then Jesus' parents brought the child in. They came to do for him what the

Law required. Simeon took Jesus in his arms and praised God. He said,

"Lord, you are the King over all.
Now let me, your servant, go in peace.
That is what you promised.
My eyes have seen your salvation.
You have prepared it in the sight of all nations.
It is a light to be given to the Gentiles.
It will be the glory of your people Israel."

The child's father and mother were amazed at what was said about him. Then Simeon blessed them. He said to Mary, Jesus' mother, "This child is going to cause many people in Israel to fall and to rise. God has sent him. But many will speak against him. The thoughts of many hearts will be known. A sword will wound your own soul too."

There was also a prophet named Anna. She was the daughter of Penuel from the tribe of Asher. Anna was very old. After getting married, she lived with her husband seven years. Then she was a widow until she was 84. She never left the temple. She worshiped night and day, praying and going without food. Anna came up to Jesus' family at that moment. She gave thanks to God. And she spoke about the child to all

who were looking forward to the time
when Jerusalem would be set free.
  Joseph and Mary did everything the Law
of the Lord required. Then they returned to
Galilee. They went to their own town of
Nazareth.

  Key Point: Mary and Joseph take Jesus to the temple to
be dedicated, and while they were there, Jesus was
recognized as the Messiah.

* Discussion: How would it make you feel to know God
  had chosen to tell you something so special and
  important as the coming of the Messiah?
* Discussion: How can we stay close to God and get to
  know Him? How can we hear God's voice?
* Discussion: If you were Mary and Joseph, would it be an
  encouragement to you to hear someone call your baby
  the Messiah? How so?

Day 27

Psalm 72:10-11

May the kings of Tarshish and of places far
away bring him gifts.
May the kings of Sheba and Seba
give him presents.
May all kings bow down to him.
May all nations serve him.

Matthew 2:1-12

Jesus was born in Bethlehem in Judea. This
happened while Herod was king of Judea.
After Jesus' birth, Wise Men from the east
came to Jerusalem. They asked, "Where is
the child who has been born to be king of
the Jews? We saw his star when it rose.
Now we have come to worship him."
When King Herod heard about it, he was
very upset. Everyone in Jerusalem was
troubled too. 4 So Herod called together all
the chief priests of the people. He also
called the teachers of the law. He asked
them where the Messiah was going to be
born. "In Bethlehem in Judea," they
replied. "This is what the prophet has
written. He said,
"But you, Bethlehem, in the land of Judah,

are certainly not the least important among the towns of Judah. A ruler will come out of you. He will rule my people Israel like a shepherd.'

Then Herod secretly called for the Wise Men. He found out from them exactly when the star had appeared. He sent them to Bethlehem. He said, "Go and search carefully for the child. As soon as you find him, report it to me. Then I can go and worship him too."

After the Wise Men had listened to the king, they went on their way. The star they had seen when it rose went ahead of them. It finally stopped over the place where the child was. When they saw the star, they were filled with joy. The Wise Men went to the house. There they saw the child with his mother Mary. They bowed down and worshiped him. Then they opened their treasures. They gave him gold, frankincense and myrrh. But God warned them in a dream not to go back to Herod. So, they returned to their country on a different road.

Key Point: Wise men from far away learned the signs of the Messiah's coming. They traveled to find Him bringing gifts.

- Draw a picture of what you would give to Jesus or find an object to represent your gift. Tell what you would give and why you chose that gift.
- Dress up as a wise man. Find out where they came from and when they arrived and found Jesus.
- Discussion: Why was Herod so jealous of Jesus?

Day 28

Hosea 11:1

The LORD continues, "When Israel was a young nation, I loved them. I chose to bring my son out of Egypt.

Matthew 2:13-15

When the Wise Men had left, Joseph had a dream. In the dream an angel of the Lord appeared to Joseph. "Get up!" the angel said. "Take the child and his mother and escape to Egypt. Stay there until I tell you to come back. Herod is going to search for the child. He wants to kill him."

So Joseph got up. During the night, he left for Egypt with the child and his mother Mary. They stayed there until King Herod died. So, the words the Lord had spoken through the prophet came true. He had said, "I brought my son out of Egypt."

Key Point: Joseph had to take Jesus to Egypt to protect Him from Herod, another event that was predicted ahead of time.

- Using Google maps, figure out how long it would take to walk from Bethlehem to Egypt. Why did they have to leave?
- Act out the scene.

Day 29

Ezekiel 36:24-29

"I will take you out of the nations. I will gather you together from all the countries. I will bring you back into your own land. I will sprinkle pure water on you. Then you will be 'clean.' I will make you completely pure and 'clean.' I will take all the statues of your gods away from you. I will give you new hearts. I will give you a new spirit that is faithful to me. I will remove your stubborn hearts from you. I will give you hearts that obey me. I will put my Spirit in you. I will make you want to obey my rules. I want you to be careful to keep my laws. Then you will live in the land I gave your people of long ago. You will be my people. And I will be your God. I will save you from all your 'uncleanness.' I will give you plenty of grain. You will have more

than enough. So, you will never be hungry
again.

Key Point: God sent the Messiah, Jesus, to save His
people from their sins and bring them back into a
relationship with Him.

- People in the Old Testament had to sacrifice animals at
  the Temple to be forgiven of their sins. A priest had to
  help them. They had to sacrifice an animal each time
  they needed forgiveness. Compare how people in the
  Old Testament were forgiven with what Jesus did to give
  us clean hearts.
- Discussion: What is so special about what Jesus did for
  us? Have you accepted the gift of salvation from God?

Day 30

Daniel 7:13-14

"In my vision I saw one who looked like a
son of man. He was coming with the clouds
of heaven. He approached the Eternal God.
He was led right up to him. And he was
given authority, glory and a kingdom.
People of all nations, no matter what
language they spoke, worshiped him. His

authority will last forever. It will not pass away. His kingdom will never be destroyed.

Key Point: There is one part of the promises about the Messiah coming that is still unfulfilled. God promised that the Messiah would come back again and be our King forever.

- Discussion: What do you look forward to the most about being with Jesus in Heaven?
- Read Revelation chapter 21 out loud. Draw pictures of what you think Heaven will look like.

References

55 Prophecies About Jesus. (2019, 07). Retrieved from Jesus Film: jesusfilm.org

Knowing Jesus Through the Old Testament. (2014). In *Knowing Jesus Through the Old Testament (Knowing God Through the Old Testament Set).* IVP Academic.

McDowell, J. (1992). A Ready Defense. In *A Ready Defense The Best Of Josh Mcdowell* (p. Chapter 19). Thomas Nelson.

Strobel, L. (2016). The Case for Christ. In *The Case for Christ: A Journalist's Personal Investigation of the Evidence for Jesus* (p. Chapter 10). Zondervan.

Walter C. Kaiser, J. (2006, November 22). *The Promise of the Messiah.* Retrieved from Billy Graham Evangelistic Association: https://billygraham.org/decision-magazine/november-2006/the-promise-of-the-messiah/

This book is dedicated to my family. Thank you to my amazing husband, John, and my incredibly talented and supportive children, Joshua and Julianna. This book is dedicated to you since this book could not have been written without your support. I love you!

This book is also dedicated to my dear friend and mentor, Carol Jackson. Your incredible friendship and example will be missed, but never forgotten. You were a true inspiration in the writing of this book.

Acknowledgements

I would like to thank the following people for all of their help and encouragement:

Thank you, Jeannie Kern for offering your pristine editing skills and many words of encouragement.

Thank you, Bobby Gentillo, for lending your amazing production and musical talents to the music for this project.

Thank you, Isaiah Becker, for all of your musical ideas and incredible guitar skills. It was so much fun co-writing several songs together.

Thank you, Erinne Holmes, for your help in navigating the world of self-publishing.

Thank you, Jacob Francis & Julianna Williams, for your incredible work on the formatting of the book and the book cover. Your persistence and expertise were so appreciated.

Thank you, Joshua Williams, for applying your design skills to the book cover.

Thank you, Paul Gibbs and Nate Miller, with NoteSpire Music for all of your promotional work. And thank you to the Clapper family for appearing in the promotional video.

Thank you to my awesome team of proof-readers and advisors. You all rock! Thank you, Jenny Ayers, Scott Carter, Pastor Jeremy Drake, Pastor Don Heindel, Dr. Ken Read, Pastor Robert Riedy, and Julianna Williams.

Made in the USA
Lexington, KY
11 November 2019

56802934R00124